RELIGION IN TRANSITION

RELIGION IN TRANSITION

S. RADHAKRISHNAN
C. F. ANDREWS
GEORGE A. COE
ALFRED LOISY
JAMES H. LEUBA
EDWIN D. STARBUCK

Edited by

VERGILIUS FERM

ESSAY INDEX

Essay Index Reprint Series

 BOOKS FOR LIBRARIES PRESS
FREEPORT, NEW YORK

First Published 1937
Reprinted 1969

LIBRARY OF CONGRESS CATALOG CARD NUMBER:

68-29204

PRINTED IN THE UNITED STATES OF AMERICA

CONTENTS

"We to-day have reached one of those crises in history when old institutions, ideals, and habits are being cracked and shattered by the upthrusting force of the superhuman growth of meaning and value. But these meanings and values cannot be consummated in the experience of human living until this old obstructive debris is taken out of the way. Such is the present state of society. In face of such a situation anyone who thinks that God will do it all and man has nothing to do, is wrapped in a blanket of delusion. It may be that men will refuse to do this work. If so, it will never be done and the great opportunity of this age to experience a superhuman flowering of meaning and value, will pass. In that case future historians will say: A springtime of history hovered near and then departed. After that winter came."

WIEMAN AND WIEMAN
Normative Psychology of Religion

EDITOR'S PREFACE

IN an age so convulsed as ours it is fitting that there be recorded some first-hand experiences of its storm and stress by those who are living creatively and prophetically. Few ages have seen such rapid transitions of thought and practice as ours; and no age has furnished more interesting biographical material than the one which casts into its framework personalities now in their prime. In the religious area of thought and action the maelstrom is no less in evidence; future generations will hardly witness such spectacular revolutions of religious thought as have been witnessed by those who are still living, especially by those whose lives touch both centuries.

A few years ago, under the title of *Contemporary American Theology*, there was published in two volumes the intimately confessional stories of some twenty leaders of contemporary religious and theological thought. The very warm reception given to that undertaking has given encouragement to the present project. It was felt that in such an important era as ours, where the pioneering spirit is so strikingly called into play, intimate personal experiences of some of those whose work has wider connotations than that covered by the term "theological" should find a place of recording, of persons who have in the storm and stress of change found themselves turning over fresh soil and marking out new paths in fields closely

related to religious philosophy and theology: fields
such as the psychology of religion, religious education,
character education, missionary enterprise, religion
interpreted as an expression of the total culture, the
rapprochement of Eastern and Western thought,
classic Catholicism in conflict with modernism, and
the like. Plenty of books have appeared setting forth
the story of these conflicts and changes; a scant few
have given the stories by the men themselves, by those
who already are widely recognized as having given a
sense of direction for the future. It was felt, too, that
such a recording should not be limited to national
borders, but rather to be more international in
character.

The editor, accordingly, has approached a few of
the leaders in these wider fields and asked for their
stories. It has not been so easy to gather these essays
together. The most difficult, partly perhaps because
the most delicate, type of writing is autobiography.
Only dogged persistence and the assurance that there
is a wide circle of readers who would welcome a word
of self-revelation from those whose names are so well
known, not to say of those of a later age who shall
be studying present-day transitional thought, have
made such a book as this possible.

Were one to list the pioneers in the twentieth-
century born science of religious psychology, one
would unhesitatingly name the three whose life stories
appear in this volume, Coe, Leuba, and Starbuck.
Were one to mention the names of those whose
researches have opened up new vistas in the fields of

religious education and so-called character education, one would think of George Albert Coe and Edwin Diller Starbuck. Were one to mention the names of those who have undertaken a new type of missionary enterprise, one would include the name of C. F. Andrews. Were one to select two or three men who in a very conspicuous way are trying to bring Eastern and Western thought into some kind of alliance and who are trying to reinterpret Western thought to Easterners and Eastern thought to Westerners, one would list the name of S. Radhakrishnan. Were one to name an outstanding Catholic modernist who has boldly espoused the cause of an enfranchised thought amidst ancient and hallowed surroundings, one would call to mind without any hesitation the name of Alfred Loisy. Were one to give the names of those who think of religion as a part of the total culture and intimately bound up with social implications on a grand scale, one would have a list long indeed; included in such a list one would set down such representative leaders in religious thought and action as are here presented. All these names have become household names among those who are well informed.

These men are here to tell in the briefest manner the story of their religious gropings in an age of transition; and in so far as they do this they are very directly characterizing the age through which we are passing. To follow their stories is to understand in a more intimate manner the thought and practice of our present day in areas religious, social, educational, political, and cultural. It has been urged upon them that they speak unhesitatingly about themselves: the books which they have read and which have placed a mark upon them, their teachers, their contemporaries in agreement and controversy, their contacts in general. Above all, they have been asked to record the factors which have played into their change of outlook and to be prophetic about what they believe is still around the corner.

Though this book is about them we hope the general reader will not miss the point that the book is also about ourselves. An autobiographical picture is never an isolated photograph; it is always a commentary.   VERGILIUS FERM

THE COLLEGE OF WOOSTER

WOOSTER, OHIO, U.S.A.

ACKNOWLEDGMENT

I WISH to acknowledge with warm appreciation the kindness of Miss M. D. Petre, of Sussex, England, in consenting to do the English translation of Professor Loisy's essay for this volume.

Thomas Y. Crowell Company, of New York, have kindly given their permission for the use of the extract on Page 6 from *Normative Psychology of Religion*.   THE EDITOR

My Search for Truth

by

S. RADHAKRISHNAN

1. EARLY YEARS

I WAS born on September 5, 1888, at a small place,
Tirutani, forty miles to the north-west of Madras,
in South India, the second child of Hindu parents,
who were conventional in their religious outlook.
I have not had any advantages of birth or of wealth.
The early years of my life till twelve were spent in
Tirutani and Tirupati, both famous as pilgrim centres.
I cannot account for the fact that from the time I
knew myself I have had firm faith in the reality of
an unseen world behind the flux of phenomena, a
world which we apprehend not with the senses but
with the mind, and even when I was faced by grave
difficulties, this faith has remained unshaken. A medi-
tative frame of mind is perhaps responsible for my
love of loneliness. Side by side with my outward
activities, there is in me an inner life of increasing
solitude in which I love to linger. Books, the vistas
they unveil, and the dreams they awaken, have been
from the beginning my constant and unfailing companions. I am not quite at home in the conventional
social functions by which life's troubles are tem-

pered to most of us. When I am in company, unless it be with one or two who know me well, it is with an effort that I get along. But I have an almost uncanny knack of putting myself *en rapport* with any individual, high or low, old or young, if the need arises. While I am essentially shy and lonely, I pass for a social and sociable man. My withdrawn nature and social timidity have given me a reputation that I am difficult to know. Again, I am said to be cold and strong-willed, while I know that I am the opposite of it. I am capable of strong and profound emotions, which I generally tend to conceal. I am nervously organized, sensitive, and highstrung. If with an unstable, sensitive nature and ordinary intellectual gifts I have not yet made a mess of this life, and if the editor thinks it worth his while to ask me to contribute an autobiographical essay to this volume, it is due to good luck. When Napoleon's eagle eye flashed down the list of officers proposed for promotion to higher rank, he used to scribble in the margin of a name "Is he lucky?" I have luck, and it is this that has protected me thus far. It is as if a great pilot had been steering my ship through the innumerable rocks and shoals on which other barks had made shipwreck. The major decisions of my life have been taken under a sort of guidance. I think, plan, and prepare, and yet when the choice is made, I have a feeling that an invisible hand has been guiding me for purposes other than my own. I do not, however, pretend that

I enjoy the special care of providence. Such a feeling, if it means more than the simple truth that the Supreme has an individual interest in and a delicate care for human beings, that its love is individual, immediate, and intimate, is an irrational prejudice. While I attribute the little success I have achieved to this luck or guidance, I do not want to shift the blame for my failures to ill luck or circumstances. My achievements are not entirely my own, but my mistakes are in large part due to my own folly or weakness.

II. HOME LIFE

I have often been reminded in later years of Hegel's saying that a man has made up his account with this life when he has work that suits him and a wife whom he loves. While men fill their feverish days with politics and business, love affairs and worldly careers, and drain to its dregs the enchanting cup of life, women, who are less sophisticated and so closer to reality, perceive that the true meaning of life is not exhausted by its obvious routine. They cling to the deeper and more ultimate reality in the light of which life no longer seems contingent and mediocre. In the battle between the naturalists and the idealists, between those who affirm that only those things are real which can be touched and handled, and those who believe, in addition, in the reality of eternal values, the women of India are found conspicuously fighting on the side of the latter. By example rather than by precept, by their life rather than by their words, they lend an importance and depth of meaning to the passing events which form so large a part of our daily life. Though many of my class and generation were married earlier than it is usual in Western countries, these early marriages were not unsuccessful. The Hindu ideal of a wife, exalted and exacting, still has a strong hold on unsophisticated Hindu women. "If he is faithless, I must be faithful. If he is shaken, I must abide. If he seeks another, I must await his return." If there is a taint in this blind devotion, then there is a taint in the Eternal who loves us with the same love, awaiting us patient and un-wearied, when we return, weary with false pleasures, to him. A pure unquestioning love that triumphs over the weaknesses of the loved one is perhaps the greatest gift of heaven. Full of tenderness and deep affection as Indian married life is, its value can be greatly increased by suitable changes in the social institutions which have become stabilized by the unwillingness of legislatures to interfere with social customs. The only security which Indian women have against the breaking of their bodies and minds is the good will of their husbands and this is not enough in our present conditions.

III. PHILOSOPHY AND RELIGION

I had my school and college career in Christian missionary institutions.[1] At an impressionable period of my life, I became familiar not only with the teaching of the New Testament, but with the criticisms levelled by Christian missionaries on Hindu beliefs and practices. My pride as a Hindu roused by the enterprise and eloquence of Swāmi Vivekānanda was deeply hurt by the treatment accorded to Hinduism in missionary institutions. It was difficult for me to concede that Hindu ascetics and teachers who preserved for our world a living contact with the classical culture of India, which is at the root of much that we know and almost all that we practise, were not truly religious. Even the poor illiterate villagers with their ancient household traditions and religious observances seemed to me to be more familiar with the spiritual mystery enveloping this world than the emancipated, comfort-minded intellectuals eager for life and adventure. They were aware of the ancient truths and maxims which the spectacle of human life has suggested to thinking minds in all ages. Life is short and happiness uncertain. Death comes to all, prince and peasant alike. True knowledge is to know one's

[1] I was in the German Mission High School, Tirupati (1896–1900), Voorhees' College, Vellore (1901–4), and Madras Christian College (1905–9).

own ignorance. Contentment is better than riches, and a mind at peace with itself is worth more than the applause of assemblies. The superstitious Indian woman may have her haunting fears but, thanks to centuries of training, she has a noble dignity, a tender refinement and a mental poise and magnanimity which many of her more intellectual contemporaries lack. The village pilgrim who spends all his earnings to have a bath in the Ganges or a darsán of the deity at Puri, who undertakes weary marches through toil and suffering to Benares or Kailas, has an innate conviction that man does not live by bread alone. Our age is a sophisticated one. In its superior fashion it laughs at gods and ghosts, values and ideals. It is too clever to take these outworn superstitions seriously, but the illiterate Hindus who are foolish enough to perceive that these things are the symbols of thoughts beyond the reach of our rational minds do not merit our derision. I know that the people of India are the victims of paralysing superstitions, but I cannot believe that they are devoid of religious sense. Every mother teaches her child that if he is to grow up religiously, he must love God, abstain from sin, and be full of sympathy and help to those who are in trouble. We have invented innumerable ways of spending the time allotted to us. May it not be that the way of the primitive Hindu is not the least wise of these? To dwell on the contemplation of eternal ideas, to struggle to behold the divine with the eye of the mind and to feed on the shadows of perfection, is that an ignoble life?

My religious sense did not allow me to speak a rash or a profane word of anything which the soul of man holds or has held sacred. This attitude of respect for all creeds, this elementary good manners in matters of spirit, is bred into the marrow of one's bones by the Hindu tradition, by its experience of centuries. Religious tolerance marked the Hindu culture from its very beginnings. When the Vedic Aryans came into contact with people professing other creeds, they soon adjusted themselves to the new elements. The Vedic religion received incalculable material and impulse for the determining of its own unique character through the re-shaping of its foreign elements. The famous Hindu scripture, *Bhagavadgītā*, declares that if one has faith and devotion to the other gods, it is faith and devotion to the supreme One, though not in the prescribed way.[1] The end of religion is an essential knowledge of God. Doctrines about God are only guides to the seekers who have not reached the end. They represent God under certain images, as possessing certain attributes and not as He is in himself. For example, in Christendom, God the Father gave place to God the Mother in the Middle Ages as in Mariolatry when she was said to be "Queen of Heaven, who can do all that she wills."[2] No formula

[1] ix. 23.
[2] Dante, *Paradiso*, xxiii. 34.

B

can confine God.[1] Besides, the knowledge we are capable of receiving depends on the stage of our development. A great truth cannot be imparted to one who possesses a narrower one answering to the measure of his capacity. If the life is deepened, the imperfect truth gives place to the more perfect one. The true teacher helps us to deepen our insight, not alter our view. He gives us a better access to our own scriptures, for "the path men take from every side is mine."[2] The different religions are not rival or competing forces, but fellow labourers in the same great task. God has not left Himself without witness among any people. Clement of Alexandria allows that there was always a natural manifestation of the one Almighty God amongst all right-thinking men.[3] Bred in such beliefs, I was somewhat annoyed that truly religious people—as many Christian missionaries undoubtedly were—could treat as subjects for derision doctrines that others held in deepest reverence. This unfortunate practice has, in my opinion, little support in the teaching or example of Jesus, though some of his later followers encouraged it. Religious truth outside the Biblical revelation was according to Augustine a work of the devil, a caricature perpetrated by demons.[4] Serious students of

[1] Cp. Some seek a Father in the heavens above;
Some ask a human image to adore;
Some crave a spirit vast as life and love;
Within thy mansions we have all and more.
[2] *Bhagavadgītā*, iv. 11. [3] Misc. Book V.
[4] Mohammed believed that the jinns stole parts of what was said in heaven. *Qurán*, 37.7 ff.

comparative religion are impressed by the general revelation of God. All truth about God has its source in God. The conception of a unique revelation, of a chosen people is contrary to the love and justice of God. It is a pet fancy of the pious that their own religion is the flower of the development of religion, its final end into which all others converge. In the new world order such a view of spiritual monopolies has no place.

The challenge of Christian critics impelled me to make a study of Hinduism and find out what is living and what is dead in it. The spirit of the times, in which India, so to say, was turning in its sleep, strengthened this resolve. The philosophy courses for the B.A. and the M.A. degrees in the Madras University did not demand any acquaintance with the Indian systems of thought and religion. Even to-day Indian philosophy forms a very minor part of philosophical studies in Indian Universities. In partial fulfilment of the conditions for the M.A. degree examination, I prepared a thesis on the *Ethics of the Vedānta*, which was intended to be a reply to the charge that the Vedānta system had no room for ethics. At the time (1908) when I was only a young student of twenty, the publication of a book with my name on the title-page excited me a great deal, though now, when I look back upon the juvenile and rhetorical production, I am ashamed that I ever wrote it. My great surprise, however, was that my distinguished teacher, Professor A. G. Hogg, the present

Principal of the Madras Christian College, a thinker of great penetration in theological matters, awarded me a testimonial, which I still treasure, in which he expressed himself thus: "The thesis which he prepared in the second year of his study for this degree shows a remarkable understanding of the main aspects of the philosophical problem, a capacity for handling easily a complex argument besides more than the average mastery of good English." All the same, that little essay indicates the general trend of my thought. Religion must establish itself as a rational way of living. If ever the spirit is to be at home in this world and not merely a prisoner or a fugitive, secular foundations must be laid deep and preserved worthily. Religion must express itself in reasonable thought, fruitful action, and right social institutions.

From April 1909, when I was appointed to the Department of Philosophy in the Madras Presidency College, I have been a teacher of philosophy and engaged in the serious study of Indian philosophy and religion. I soon became convinced that religion is an autonomous form of experience which cannot be confused with anything else, not even with morality, though it cannot help expressing itself in a high code of morality. Religion is essentially a concern of the inner life. Its end is to secure spiritual certainty which lifts life above meaningless existence or dull despair. It must be judged by its own standard, whether it gives security to values, meaning to life, confidence to adventure. Its roots lie in the spirit of man, deeper

than feeling, will or intellect. The deepest depths of
the soul reflect the divine, when they are kept un-
dimmed. "God has put eternity into the heart of man,"
says the Preacher. The sense of the infinite is the basis
of religion. This sense is not satisfied with what the
eyes see or the ears hear. When cultivated, it introduces
us into a higher world than the material. A man may
be highly moral, practise virtue scrupulously, but if
faith and hope in the spiritual direction of the universe
are not there, he is not a religious man. Religion is
that knowledge of the essential nature of reality, that
insight or penetration which satisfies not only a more
or less powerful intellectual impulse in us, but that
which gives to our very being the point of contact
which it needs for its vital power, for the realization
of its true dignity, for its saving. To this end intense
spiritual labour and moral activity are needed. To have
a vision of God requires a pure heart. To know the
truth, not learning but the heart of a child is needed.
The ethical has a prominent place in the process of
the purification of the mind by which communion
with God is brought about. When the goal is reached,
the spirit shines through and illuminates the whole
life, filling it with ethical character and vital energy.

Whatever may be the Hindu practice, Hindu religion cannot be regarded as unworldly or other-worldly.
According to it, the aim of religion is to attain a knowledge or a vision of God and the aim of ethics is to
remake human life into the mould of the unseen.
The two are bound up with each other. The conscious-

ness of the infinite spirit is the impulse to the ideal. It expresses itself in a burning passion for righteousness and purity. The sense of the spiritual and the longing for righteousness go together.

A verse in the *Mahābhārata* says that the mark of the Aryan is not learning, not religion, but conduct alone. Philosophy in India is not an abstract study remote from the life of man. It is intimately woven into the texture of human existence. The civilization of India is an effort to embody philosophical wisdom in social life. My occasional contributions to learned magazines like the *International Journal of Ethics*, *Monist*, *Quest*, had for their objective the establishing of the ethical character of the Hindu religion. Spiritual values are realized on earth through the empiric means of family love, of love and friendship, of loyalty and reverence. To the truly religious, all life is a sacrament. Modern attempts to improve the general condition of the community, to transform society so that hope and happiness might be brought within the reach of the needy and the downtrodden, are not inconsistent with the Hindu religion but are demanded by it.

It is urged often that belief in the illusory character of the world associated with the Hindu religion conflicts with ethical seriousness. It is wrong to interpret the meaning of the doctrine of māyā in a way that affects the urgency of the ethical demand. The doctrine of māyā declares that the world is dependent on and derived from the ultimate reality. It has the character of perpetual passing away, while the real is exempt from change. It has therefore a lower status than the supreme itself. In no case is its existence to be confused with illusory being or non-existence. Even Śaṁkara, who advocates the theory of māyā, carefully distinguishes the phenomenal existence of the world from the being of Brahman and the non-being of dreams, illusions, etc. Besides, many other interpreters of the Vedānta repudiate the doctrine of māyā even in this limited sense.

In regard to my views on Hindu ethics and the doctrine of māyā, I found great support in the writings of Rabindranath Tagore. The results of my study of his works (translated into English) are embodied in a book which Macmillan (London) brought out in 1918. This book, which has all the faults of immature youth, secured on the whole a friendly reception. The poet himself was extremely generous. He wrote in December 1918: "Though my criticism of a book that concerns me may not be seriously accepted, I can say that it has surpassed my expectation. The earnestness of your endeavour and your penetration have amazed me, and I am thankful to you for the literary grace of its language which is so beautifully free from all technical jargon and a mere display of scholarship."

In 1918 I was appointed Professor of Philosophy in the new University of Mysore. My previous studies inclined me to accept a spiritual, non-dogmatic view of religion. It is not a private revelation or what is imposed by public authority, but what springs naturally from the light of reason and the insight of experience. I was persuaded that philosophy led us to a spiritual or, what I then called, an absolutist view of religion. If philosophy is employed to lend support to a pluralistic idealism which looks upon God as the President of the Immortals and human individuals as eternal spirits who will retain for all time their unique irreplaceable significance, it is influenced by our religious prepossessions. I published a series of articles in *Mind* on M. Bergson's philosophy, pointing out that he was an absolutist. From a similar standpoint I examined the philosophical views of Leibniz, James Ward, William James, Rudolf Eucken, Hastings Rashdall, Bertrand Russell, Lord Balfour, etc., and pointed out that their implicit support of pluralism or pluralistic theism is traceable to the interference of religion with the pursuit of philosophy. This thesis was set forth in an ambitious work on *The Reign of Religion in Contemporary Philosophy* (Macmillan, 1920). It had a very warm reception. Noted critics praised it beyonds its merits. Apart from many favourable reviews by men of established reputation in philosophy like J. H. Muirhead, J. S. Mackenzie, and J. E. C. McTaggart, among others, Professor Hinman of America in his presidential address to the American Philosophical Association selected for treatment "Two Representative Idealists, Bosanquet and Radhakrishnan."[1] To be coupled with Bosanquet is an honour which more eminent men would covet. The book was

---

[1] See *Philosophical Review*, 1921, pp. 333–51, also 1920, pp. 582–6.

used by students in metaphysics not only in Indian universities, but in several British and American ones, and I became somewhat known as a writer on philosophy.

In 1921 I was appointed to the most important philosophy chair in India, King George V Chair of Mental and Moral Science in the University of Calcutta. Professor J. H. Muirhead, to whom I owe more than I can tell, invited me to write a systematic and readable account of Indian philosophy for his famous "Library of Philosophy." I put together my studies on this subject, which occupied me from 1908, and published the two volumes which are now in their second edition. The task of bringing together a multitude of minute particulars into a creative and cumulative relationship is not an easy one. My ambition in this work was not only to chronicle but to interpret, to show the interconnection of the different views, to render the vibration of life. Besides, in all philosophical interpretation the right method is to interpret thinkers at their best, in the light of what they say in their moments of clearest insight. There is no reason why philosophical writers should not be judged as other creative artists are, at least in the main, on the basis of their finest inspirations. To understand a great thinker, we must have enough sympathy to imagine ourselves as standing in his place, possessing his information, cherishing his beliefs, feeling his emotions. So long as we keep reminding ourselves that we are modern and that these ancients had faults and passions that we do not share, we can never achieve more than caricatures of these thinkers. Humility is the mother of all writing, even though that writing may relate to the history of philosophy. I am happy that I helped, to some extent, in the endeavour to take Hindu thought again into the general stream of human thought. There was a time when it was regarded as something quaint, strange, antiquated, incapable of playing a part in the world's spiritual awakening. But that impression is slowly disappearing. Ancient Indians do not belong to a different species from ourselves. We find from an actual study of their views that they ask questions and find answers analogous in their diversity to some of the more important currents in modern thought. Indian philosophy is now recognized as an important branch of study and even the editors of the *Encyclopaedia Britannica* (fourteenth edition) found some space for it and asked me to write the article on "Indian Philosophy."

Through my articles in the *Hibbert Journal*, I was brought into contact with its editor, Dr. L. P. Jacks, late Principal of Manchester College, Oxford, who graciously invited me to give the Upton Lectures on *The Hindu View of Life*, in 1926, in his college. I was enabled to accept his invitation, as the University of Calcutta deputed me to represent it at the Congress of the Universities of the British Empire in June 1926, and the International Congress of Philosophy at the Harvard University in September 1926. This was my first visit to Europe and America and I have the most pleasant recollections of it. The very warm reception which I had in Oxford and Cambridge, in Harvard and Princeton, in Yale and Chicago, and many other places, is fixed in my mind.

In the lectures on *The Hindu View of Life*[1] I represent Hinduism as a progressive historical movement still in the making. Its adherents are not custodians of a deposit, but runners carrying a lighted torch. The weaknesses of the Hindu faith which have drawn the institution into disgrace and are to-day blocking the way for social advance are due to a confusion between tradition and truth. We must preserve the spirit of truth which will guide us into all truth. God does not say "I am Tradition," but He says "I am Truth." Truth is greater than its greatest teachers. We must realize that the history of the race is strewn with customs and institutions which were invaluable at first and deadly afterwards. Gross abuses which still survive require to be cut off with an unsparing hand. Hinduism insists on the upward striving, not only in the sphere of morals but in that of intellect. It is not to be regarded as either pessimistic or fatalistic. The law of karma affirms the implicit presence of the past in the present. When we unconsciously or mechanically follow the impulses of the past, we are not exercising our freedom. But we are free when our personal subject becomes the ruling centre. It is not necessary for me to refer to the different criticisms

[1] George Allen & Unwin, London. Fourth Impression, Macmillan & Co., New York.

urged against the Hindu faith since the chief of them are considered in that book.

At the Philosophical Congress held at Harvard University in September 1926, the lack of spiritual note in modern civilization was the theme of my address to the general meeting, an idea which I set forth in some detail in a small book called *Kalki, or the Future of Civilization*.[1] In the last few decades the world has been transformed so rapidly and completely at any rate in its superficial aspects. Science helps us to build up our outer life, but another discipline is necessary to strengthen and refine the living spirit. Though we have made enormous progress in knowledge and scientific inventions, we are not above the level of past generations in ethical and spiritual life. In some respects we have perhaps declined from their standards. Our natures are becoming mechanized; void within, we are reduced to mere atoms in a community, members of a mob. Behaviourist psychology teaches us that man has no inwardness and can be understood completely from the standpoint of the observer.

Some of the recent attempts at the replanning of society are attended with this danger. Though man has compelled the world to minister to his needs, though the application of modern science to production and distribution enables us to provide the possibilities of material well-being for all and make

[1] Messrs. Kegan Paul published it in their "To-day and To-morrow" series, 1928. Second edition, 1934.

poverty an anachronism, still large numbers of men are suffering from poverty and starvation. This chaotic condition is due to a lack of fellowship and co-operation. The Russian experiment, whatever we may think of it, is at least an honest attempt to secure for all an equal share in things which constitute the physical basis of life. The glaring contrasts of poverty and wealth are not accepted by them as inevitable. Even Fascism is labouring to build up a true communal life and effect a more equitable distribution of power, wealth, and opportunity. Only the unfortunate result of these attempts is mutual conflict and suppression of individual liberty. There is a standardization of souls, a loss of self-confidence, a tendency to seek salvation in herds. Not only is the individual robbed of his freedom to order his life as he wills, he is also deprived of the liberty to think as he will and express his thoughts and opinions. Society has become a prison. That there is a real feeling for humanity in these desperate attempts to check the economic exploitation of the masses, one can readily admit. But if it is to be achieved by the other exploitation of the baser passions of human nature, its selfishness and hatred, its insolence and fanaticism, the ideal order will be an inhuman one. Let us by all means establish a just economic order, but let us also note that the economic man is not the whole man. For a complete human being, we require the cultivation of the grace and joy of souls overflowing in love and devotion and free service of a regenerated humanity. If we wish to realize the reign of law and justice in this world, it is to enable the soul to gain inward peace. Physical efficiency and intellectual alertness are dangerous if spiritual illiteracy prevails. Aldous Huxley's *Brave New World* gives us a picture of perfect adaptation of means to ends which will mean at the same time the breeding of men and women in bottles, the disappearance of all family life, of art and literature, of philosophy and religion, the death of all things of the spirit. The elimination of the inner world of personal experience is not a sign of progress. The present crisis of civilization is the direct result of the loosening hold of ethical and spiritual ideals.

We see things happening in the civilized world to-day that recall the worst phases of the dark ages. New gods of race and nation are set up in the place of God who is dethroned. The souls of men are poisoned and perverted by collective myths. They control their loyalties, present apocalyptic hopes, demand an intense and passionate devotion to a goal outside and greater than the self and serve as religions which have the power to give luminous meaning to life and stir the will to action. The few who have the perception of the unity of mankind and feel the happiness and misery of a neighbouring people as though it were their own are swamped by the millions who are taught to accustom themselves to the idea of humanity as an assemblage of combatant communities whose strength is tested through war. The

not take account of the movement of mind, the
stream of ideas, the pace and direction in which life
and time are flowing. Dynamic and ambitious nations
eager to effect changes in the *status quo* withdraw
from the League to resume unrestrained liberty of
political action. They declare that justice comes first
and peace second. The League consists of the satisfied
powers and the weaker nations.

More than the economic factor, the psychological
element of prestige operates in the matter of the
possession of colonies. While they are for their
owners a source of profit, they provoke the envious
resentment of others. The determination of some
nations to hold on to what they have and defend it
at all costs, and the equal determination of others to
wrest it from them, are the causes of wars. If only
the great powers are willing to make in advance a
small part of the sacrifices which each of them will
have to make, should a war start, the terrible menace
which threatens us to-day could be warded off. The
lead in this matter can be taken by Great Britain,
whose political realism is not unmixed with idealism.
Britain is aiming at transforming its empire into a
free partnership of nations which enter into it of
voluntary accord. The inferior status of India in it
is a source of weakness and makes it an object of
envy to others. So long as India is a dependency and
not a dominion, Great Britain cannot complain if
Italy and Germany wish to take their share in what
the Britisher in other moods called the white man's
burden. She has no moral authority to question

C

Japan's adventures in the Far East or Italy's in Africa. Things are never settled until they are settled right. If we go behind the give and take of politics to the ultimate question of right and wrong, we see that the instability of the world is due to the outrage on the moral law in which powerful nations are acquiescing. It is time we restore the supremacy of law and organize the world for an enduring peace.

Civilization is an act of spirit, not of body or of mind. Achievements of knowledge and power are not enough; acts of spirit and morality are essential. Man must become an active, purposeful force. He must cease to believe in an automatic law of progress which will realize itself irrespective of human ideals and control. Man is not a detached spectator of a progress immanent in human history, but an active agent remoulding the world nearer to his ideals. Every age is much what we choose to make it. The trouble with our civilization is that in our anxiety to pursue the things of time, we are neglecting the things are are not of time, the enduring and the eternal. The significance of man's life is not exhausted by his service of the earthly kingdom. The whole complex range of human life becomes shallow, aimless, and unsatisfying if it is not shot through with a sense of the eternal. We must build all relationships on a basis of understanding fellowship, remembering the controlling principle that life on earth is meaningless apart from its eternal background. Growth of civilization is marked by an increase of genuineness, sincerity, and unselfishness. The only effective way of altering society is the hard and slow one of changing individuals. If we put first things first, through patient effort and struggle, we will win power over circumstances and mould them. Only a humanity that strives after ethical and spiritual ideals can use the great triumphs of scientific knowledge for the true ends of civilization.

I had an opportunity of expressing this view in its philosophical setting when in 1929 I was invited to take the post vacated by Principal J. Estlin Carpenter in Manchester College, Oxford. This invitation gave me an opportunity to lecture to the students of the University of Oxford on Comparative Religion. During this visit, I had the privilege of giving the Hibbert Lectures on *An Idealist View of Life* to large audiences at the Universities of London and of Manchester. These lectures state my views on some of the ultimate problems of philosophy. They take into account the changes in the intellectual climate of the world, the crisis through which religion and social life are passing. The days of external ceremonial religion which can co-exist with a deceitful paganism are over. Men are asking for reality in religion. They want to penetrate to the depths of life, tear away the veils that hide the primordial reality and learn what is essential for life, for truth, and righteousness. The decay of dogmatic, mechanical religion led to the rise of a number of substitutes or modes of escape, but they do not show an adequate appreciation of the natural profundity of the human soul. Secular wisdom is not a substitute for religion.

Modern civilization seemed to me to suffer from the same defect of being soulless. Politics and economics do not take their direction from ethics and religion. If the lost "soul" is to be restored to human life, a new vital religion which does not require us to surrender the rights of reason, which even wholly free and disillusioned spirits can adopt, must be developed.

Religion is not a creed or a code but an insight into reality. If we confuse it with an intellectual view, we will justify the ancient practice of armed societies fighting for different versions of God's nature. The founders of religion, the saints and sages, have all been prophet souls, who had direct acquaintance with spiritual reality, in and behind that which our senses perceive.

Spiritual certainty is conveyed by spiritual knowledge, which is not merely perceptual or conceptual. This knowledge is not a-logical but super-logical. It is called integral insight or intuitive knowledge. Hegel and the rationalists are not quite right in giving the supreme position to reason in the sense of critical intelligence. The drift of our age and its ruling methods of work support a scientific rationalism. The demands of our civilization direct the attention of its workers so energetically and exclusively to that which is nearest at hand, to the investigation and practical application of our material resources. Such intensive concentration on the empirical and the technical is perhaps unique in the history of civilization. That it has benefited mankind enormously is beyond question. But even those who adopt the methods and conceptions of exact and descriptive sciences are obliged to raise the further question of the limitations and value of scientific knowledge itself. While the theories of science are useful as tools for the control of nature, they cannot be said to reveal what reality is. Electrons and protons do not clear up the mystery of reality. Besides, God and soul cannot be treated as mathematical equations. Our deepest convictions, for which we are sometimes willing to die, are not the results of rational calculation. The decisive experiences of personal life cannot be comprehended in formulas. Their driving power is in those urgent and intimate contacts with reality which convey to us deep certainties which transform our lives. Even a scientific rationalism requires us to admit the actuality of such experiences, and the phenomenal and incomplete character of merely scientific knowledge. The fact of this integral or intuitive knowledge tells us that we are not helplessly shut out from an insight into reality by the constitution of our minds.

The whole course of Hindu philosophy is a continuous affirmation of the truth that insight into reality does not come through analytical intellect, though it is accessible to the human mind in its integrality. In this conviction Hindu thinkers are supported by many others, including Plato and Plotinus, St. Paul and St. Augustine, Luther and Pascal. The very nature of the cosmic process as a perpetual creation of novelty, which is adopted by modern science, points to the need of intuition. Life is not a simple geometrical pattern. The essence of life is creativity. It is a living creation of something new, not a dead connection of cause and effect. The inner compulsion which lies behind that which is visible to our eyes is an urge to create, to generate, to make alive, to bring forth something new out of the hidden treasure of being. We shall never be able to analyse the sources of the creative spirit. If the real is a genuine becoming, then the highest knowledge can only be an insight. Yet there is enough of rationality in this insight. There is no such thing as chance in the world. There is no break in the chain of real connection, though our limited vision may not be able to penetrate to the series of causes and effects. The world is creative activity but a continuous one and a rational one. While the rationality of the world is transparent to the intellect, its mysteriousness can be grasped only by intuition.

Intuitive knowledge, however, is not opposed to intellectual knowledge as Bergson sometimes makes us believe. Intuition is not a sensual thrill or an emotional debauch. In intuitive knowledge, intellect plays a considerable part. If intuition is unsupported by intellect, it will lapse into self-satisfied obscurantism. Intuition assumes the continuity and unity of all experience. An intellectual search for the ultimate cause may lead us to an idea of God. Intuition tells us that the idea is not merely an idea but a fact. The prophet souls, the religious geniuses intuit cosmic truths which cannot be communicated except imperfectly. The intellectual creeds are such imperfect expressions and therefore sometimes seem to be conflicting one with another.

The end of man is to let the spirit in him permeate his whole being, his soul, flesh, and affections. He attains his deepest self by losing his selfish ego. Man is not a mere sum of his instincts and desires. He seeks to be a single indivisible unity or organism. Dissatisfaction and unrest accompany every breach in organic wholeness. There is always a tension between what we are and what we wish to become. The human self is a temporary unstable organization oscillating between the matter which offers the possibility of existence and the spirit which moulds it into significant being. It strives after integration.

Integrated lives are the saved ones. They possess the joy unspeakable, the peace that passeth understanding. Our earthly joys would pale before that spiritual bliss like electric lamps before the morning sun.

The new society will be built by those who have deepened their personalities and integrated their lives. The imperfect social order is a challenge to those who have achieved inner strength and integrity. They by their self-sacrificing will contribute to the reign of God, of love and of virtue on earth. No individual is really saved until society is perfected.

If the historical process is a burden from which the soul attempts to free itself, it can free itself only when the historical process reaches its fulfilment. The stronger individuals help the weaker ones until all are saved. Universal salvation is the aim of the historical process, and when the goal is reached the process disappears. The temporal becomes the eternal.

During the course of history, which is the translation of one specific possibility of the Infinite Spirit, the latter is envisaged by us as the Divine principle controlling the course of this historical succession. God is not the great silent sea of infinity in which the individuals lose themselves, but the Divine person who inspires the process first, last, and without ceasing. To say that God created the world is an understatement. He is creating now and for all time. History is in this sense the epic of the Divine will, a revelation of God. The Divine works and shines through the earthly medium. In Hindu religion the Divine is said to be the Kavi or the Poet, the maker or the creator. God as person is deeply concerned in the affairs of this world. He is the friend, judge, and the redeemer of mankind. God is the Absolute spirit, timeless and unchanging, from the cosmic or human end. He is the way in which the Absolute not only appears to and is known by us, but also the way in which it works in the cosmic process. The Absolute is at once the sum and source of limitless possibilities. One of these possibilities is being actualized in the cosmic process. To this possibility which is in course of accomplishment, the Absolute assumes the form of a God who is guiding the world with a previous knowledge of its general plan and direction. God is not a figment of our minds. God is a real symbol of the Absolute reality, an aspect of the Absolute in its relation to this specific possibility which is being actualized. He is not a distorted reflection of the Absolute but, as Leibniz says, a phenomenon well founded in the reality. When there is a complete identity between God and the world, that is, when God's purpose is fulfilled, when all individual spirits are perfected, God Himself will relapse into the Absolute, "creation being thus at once ransomed and annulled by the cessation of the impulse to individuate." The lapse of the world does not take away from the infinite reality of the Absolute spirit.[1]

This, in brief, is the view that I set forth at some length in my Hibbert Lectures, and I am grateful for the very warm reception that they had. Distinguished philosophers of Europe and America, including Samuel Alexander and Bertrand Russell, J. H. Muirhead and J. S. Mackenzie, W. R. Inge and L. P. Jacks, Rabindranath Tagore and Sir Herbert Samuel, welcomed it in the most generous terms.

Some of the sermons and occasional addresses which

[1] Cf. the peace chant of the *Bṛhadāraṇyaka Upaniṣad:*

"Pūrṇamadah pūrṇam idam pūrṇāt pūrṇam udacyate
Pūrṇasyapūrṇam ādāya pūrṇam evāvaśiṣyate.

The Absolute is infinite and this universe is infinite. The infinite proceeds from the infinite. If we take the infinite from the infinite, what remains is the infinite alone.

I gave while I was at Oxford are brought together in a small book *East and West in Religion*.[1] The main theme of these addresses is that religion consists in doing justice, in loving mercy, and in making our fellow-creatures happy. A saint is not a stained-glass image but one who works for his fellow men and endeavours to establish a new relation of loving-kindness among them. He regards an individual's need as a sufficient claim on his generosity. We must believe in the equality of men not only in the soul but in the flesh. It is true that we cannot fall in love with a telephone directory. Love of humanity must be defined in terms of the men and women with whom we are brought into contact.

It was a great experience for me to preach from Christian pulpits in Oxford and Birmingham, in Manchester and Liverpool. It heartened me to know that my addresses were liked by Christian audiences. Referring to my sermon on *Revolution through Suffering*, an Oxford daily observed, "Though the Indian preacher had the marvellous power to weave a magic web of thought, imagination, and language, the real greatness of his sermon resides in some indefinable spiritual quality which arrests attention, moves the heart, and lifts us into an ampler air."

IV. LIFE'S PROBLEMS

Those to whom life has been kind should not accept this good fortune as a matter of course. If one is

[1] George Allen & Unwin, 1933.

allowed to lead a secure life while so many around who deserve better are confined to miserable surroundings and subjected to tragic blows, it is one's duty to think continually of those who were denied the privileges one had. My position as a teacher brought me into close relations with young men and women in the plastic years of their life. The subject of philosophy, which is not primarily utilitarian in its aim, is a great instrument of liberal education. Its aim is one of elevating man above worldliness, of making him superior to circumstances, of liberating his spirit from the thraldom of material things. Philosophy claims to implant in the minds of those who are of a nature to profit by its teachings and influence a taste for those things which the world cannot give and cannot take away. If properly pursued, it arms us against failure, against sorrow and calamity, against boredom and discouragement. It may not prepare us for success if we mean by it accumulation of material wealth. But it helps us to love those aims and ideals, the things beyond all price on which the generality of men who aim at success do not set their hearts. To form men is the object of philosophy.

In the hours I was privileged to spend with my pupils, it was my ambition to educate them to a belief in a spiritual and ethical universe. If the central truths of mysticism and charity, inwardness and love are brought home to our hearts and thoughts, the temptations to irreligion which assail us in later life will have little power to overcome us. It is essential to awaken in one's pupils a feeling of need for a silent hour, a time of pure refreshment for heart and spirit, for self-communion, which will help them to collect their thoughts, reassemble their personalities and find themselves. In that silence we hear the still voices of the soul with its plaintive cry of the prisoner for freedom, of the wanderer for home, the cry of the finite for the infinite. Religion is what we do with ourselves when we are alone. In every one of us is a secret shrine where no one could intrude, to which we must retire as often as possible and discover what our true self is as distinct from the appearance we present to the world outside. Most of us are self-deceivers and constant examination alone can save us. Silent communion is an essential part of all worship. The Book of Revelation has a striking phrase that, as the seer watched the angels worshipping before the throne of God, suddenly "there was silence in Heaven for the space of half an hour." The strains of music ceased; the voices of the heavenly choir were stilled. That silence was not a dead one but pulsing with life, when the angels ceased to speak but waited in silence to hear the voice of spirit. In that stillness we come close to reality, become aware of how best we could make our life an offering to the Divine.

Worship does not consist in fasts and prayers, but in the offering of a pure and contrite heart. The musk is in the deer but it thinks that the fragrance comes from outside and so hunts for it restlessly. God is in us and we have only to turn within to realize the truth. There is a Sanskrit verse which says that the thoughtless man dives into deep lakes, penetrates into jungles, ascends steep hills in search of flowers for the worship of God while the one lotus which he can offer is his own mind.[1] Man must make himself a living sacrifice. We cannot offer anything unclean or impure, maimed or mutilated to God. "The temple of God is holy which temple ye are." Out of the confusion around us we have to devise a destiny and make it manifest through all the twists and turns of accident. Otherwise life becomes a meaningless succession of irrelevant episodes unconnected with any specific purpose, springing from nothing and returning to nothing. What gives value and meaning to life is a purpose steadily pursued through the obstacles that hinder its living growth. Interest, meaning, purpose, value, are qualities given to events by the individual mind, while chance provides the occasions for the application of these values. In these silent hours of self-communion we strive to free ourselves from the suffocating routine, from the masks and mummeries of existence, cleanse our thoughts, and create within ourselves a clean heart and a single

[1] Cf. *Śivānandalahari.*

> Gabhīre kāsāre visati vijane ghoravipine
> visālesaileca bhramati kusumārtham jaḍamatih/
> Samarpyaikam cetah sarasijam umānātha bhavate,
> Sukhenāvāsthātum jana iha na jānāti kim aho//

mind. Yoga, which has for its aim the achievement of the closest correspondence between the inner mind and the outer life, uses as its means silence, meditation, self-recollection.

I have been privileged to learn that my work has not been altogether in vain. A few men and women were enabled to regard the fundamental truth as something to be absorbed into one's thought, incorporated into one's being. Only humanity which expresses itself in peace of mind and patience with all makes human life worth living, and is of more value than health or wealth. The truly great are not those who have more money or brains or higher social position. God does not think less of people because they are poor or unintelligent. What matters is whether we have been kind to others and honest and sincere with ourselves and in our intimate relations with others. People richly endowed with physical health and material possessions are seen wrestling with care and suffering. They may appear in drawing-rooms with smiles pinned to their faces while their hearts are broken with pain. They use their power and wealth to hide from themselves their real state and by concentrating on outer achievements satisfy certain of their impulses. But deep down they understand that something is amiss with them. They feel it to be a particular unkindness of the universe that no one should stick to them, that they should become estranged from their own children, that they never succeed in forming a permanent centre and that as

they grow older, they grow more and more lonely.
Soon they find that life is meaningless to them, and
their eyes show that dumb, wondering fear which we
sometimes see in the eyes of animals, indicating a
deep melancholy, an ultimate sadness. We see in their
eyes, in spite of their lively gestures and shrill voices,
a harassed look, as if this world were not their real
home, as if they had come from some far-off place
and could not get back. A nameless sadness weighs
them down and they seem to grow indifferent to
every feeling except a faint yearning to be at peace
and dead. To the eye that has learnt to read the heart,
their frivolous excitement, their gaiety and laughter
is only a mask. The fact that they are ill at ease indicates a state of unbalance. They suffer, because they
struggle to escape from the incoherent, the unmeaning,
the enslaving to coherence, significance, and freedom.
The nearer we are to the awakening, the more
desolate do we feel. The soul is laden with the sense
of guilt, of the feeling that one ought to have done
better and with a longing for liberation. The sadness
tends to set in the direction of seeking a possible
solution, a true friend, who can guide the soul, as
parents guide their children. Blessed are they that
mourn; that suffer and weep. The heart that aches
is the heart which loves. The more tender it is, the
more does it suffer. The grief of the large-hearted
is too deep even for tears. We can buy immunity
from suffering only by giving up life's greatest good,
by hardening the heart. The story of the saint with

a crown of gold has a point. When he went to heaven and saw there all the other saints wearing their jewelled crowns, while he himself was given a crown of gold without any jewels, he asked, "Why has my crown no jewels?" The angel replied, "Because you provided none. Those jewels are the tears that saints have shed on earth. You shed none." "How could I," he asked, "when I was so happy in the love of God?" "It is much," said the angel. "Here is your crown, and it is made of gold; but jewels are for those who wept." It is by suffering that we understand. The condition of true human life is to suffer pain and endure loneliness. Only those who live outward lives without being touched to their inward depths can escape suffering. Often suffering is not punishment but discipline. When the great blow falls, when we stand in our darkest hour, shocked, baffled, defeated for the moment, when life has completely lost its savour, when we are tempted to cry "O God, art thou dead?" or with one mightier, "My God, why hast thou forsaken me?" when we hear no response even to such a cry of despair, when utter silence faces us, when the foundations slip away and the world seems to be cracking all about us, we have to bear it all, face the storm, cling to hope and believe in love. All this means suffering and it is through suffering that we learn and grow. By enduring pain we show the triumph of mind over matter, and the suffering becomes a means for growth in grace. When once anchorage is secured and life disciplined, and permeated by spirit, suffering is turned into bliss. The fear of suffering gives place to the courage to suffer. The path to bliss is found to be through pain which man consents to take upon himself.

The life of each one of us touches the lives of others at many points. We draw health and strength, comfort and encouragement from our intercourse with them. There are some to whom we have never turned in vain for sympathy and help. Such people who light fires in dark rooms are the salt of the earth. All too often we take their love and friendship for granted. We do not realize how much we owe to them, though there can be no repayment for tenderness, for sympathy, for gratitude. It asks for no reward or return. Where genuine love is present, a person desires but to give, not to sell, to receive as a pure gift, not to earn. In terms of spiritual currency, love is greater than justice, who is only a blind goddess. If the beloved sees the slightest merit in it, one would give away all he has and is and be ready to be misunderstood, ridiculed, reviled, persecuted and wounded to the core. No devotion, no sacrifice, is too great. When the soul seems dead and all the world a wilderness, when our hearts are dry and brains barren, what brings us hope and solace is not analysis or criticism but love and friendship. It is these that sweep men into new courses of life. They are greater than wealth, greater than fame, far greater than culture. Even the mighty of the earth can do no more while the poorest are capable of them. They do not depend

D

on power or riches. They need neither hands nor feet. They shine through the eyes and give warmth through a word or a smile. The touch of a compassionate hand often illuminates one like a lightning-flash in the darkness. Profound influences are wrought by creative minds by a light gesture or a brief conversation. The fund of humanity and idealism, locked up in human hearts unreleased or scarcely released, is released and overflows.

This human and intimately personal life seemed to me to be more important than that of a pedantic scholar or a dull dispenser of thought. An instinct to stand by the weak and the helpless must always be an essential part of a refined nature. No man knows another. How, then, can he judge what he does not know or understand? We know only the words and actions of others. We cannot read their thoughts, their subconscious mind. We have no clue to the secret recesses of the soul, the silent passions with which their hearts are bursting. Unless a man lives through another's experience, he cannot realize what it is like. Besides, whose life is so clean, whose character is so spotless that he can sit in judgment on others? Few will escape punishment if a method of spiritual vivisection is applied to all men. Most of us find ourselves in absurd positions when some overmastering passion reduces us to unreason. We are like birds of the forest, beating our wings in vain against the bars of the cage. Judgment is what is most hateful. Jesus, when he was confronted by the woman taken in adultery, turned not from her, but from those who sought to condemn her. He was disgusted at the foulness of their minds, at the sensuousness of their souls, at the indecency of their attitude to the poor human being. In the presence of all that vileness, that cruel malignant criticism, the only thing that was real was his love.[1] Nothing shall tempt true men to feel contempt for any or superior to any. Deep down in one's heart one knows that one is quite as other men are, as futile and as human. Most men will be criminal when tempted or heroes when inspired. We are moulded into strange shapes through ignorance and circumstances. Not all men are capable of loosening themselves from organic urges which seem to master them, though man alone, among the creatures we know of, is capable of liberating himself by means of spiritual initiative from the blind primordial urges. Most of us are the slaves of our passions. When under their control it is impossible for us to see objects in their true light. We believe whatever accords with our feelings. It is therefore the duty of every genuine soul to insist on the good side and ignore the opposite. There is an unquenched spark of the divine fire in the worst villain. The secrets of eternity are found in all though they become manifest in some.

A friend of mine, who has known me well for over twenty years, made a comment rather sarcastically

[1] For an illustration of the very similar Buddhist view, see the writer's *East and West in Religion* (1933), ch. iii.

that I am incapable of indignation, that I am fool-
proof, that I suffer gladly not only fools but the
"sinful." I am afraid that this observation is not
untrue. It is not easy to know the difference between
good men and bad. Ideas may be theoretically divided
into good and bad, but not men and women, for each
of us contains, in himself or herself, in varying
degrees, the good and the bad, the high and the low,
the true and the false. Besides, society has queer
notions about right and wrong. Unorthodox personal
relationships are wrong, while acts involving whole
nations in war are right. Cruelty, treachery, and
exploitation are condoned, while loving the wrong
person not wisely but too well is condemned, though
the latter is only a misfortune, not a crime. It is
easier to make saints out of libertines than out of
prudes and pharisees. The infinite pathos of life calls
for infinite understanding. What the "sinful" need
is not abuse and criticism. They yearn to be understood; they long for a little comfort, for respect and
rest. When they stand bewildered, when their nerves
are stretched to the breaking-point by the strain of
their own misdeeds and the contempt of the world,
what they need is some one in whom they could
trust wholeheartedly. Human affection is indispensable
to them. Not compassion, which is a form of contempt, but a tender regard which can overlook
the past and help the future. There is no need to
tread the road to ruin to the end. By a change in
mental and spiritual disposition, we can check the

rapid decline and prepare for ourselves a new destiny. It depends on us whether we take the rake's line downhill to destruction or the pilgrim's progress upward. I have every confidence in the power of love to evoke the right change. The friend takes the place of an analyst, who succeeds in removing the blind urges and fixations by exposing them to view. Some are silent, because they have nothing to say; others are silent because they have no one to say it to. To a true friend, even the most perverse will pour out their hearts and thus get relieved. He is not afraid to face the dismal reality and see it as it really is. For the soul of man is essentially a lovable thing. No human being is innately wicked or incapable of improvement. No one can succeed in stifling the soul or drugging or deceiving it for all time. The best side of a human being is his real side, his true self. Such an attitude to life makes one turn a blind eye to human inertia and weakness. "Love," says St. Paul, "is never glad when others go wrong, love is gladdened by goodness, always slow to expose, always eager to believe the best, always hopeful, always patient."[1]

It is one of the hardest things to criticize the actions of those of whom we are fond, but it is what one expects and longs for from true friendship. Every time the courage is found, the bond becomes stronger. A true friend not only seeks and inquires, but probes and pierces, digs his fists into the heart, through this process of ruthless unveiling or

[1] Corinthians xiii. 6–8. Moffat's translation.

pitiless exposure is most painful and costing. But then the only way to attain peace of mind and inward harmony is by means of knowledge and adjustment. We must be completely sincere with ourselves and then adjust ourselves to circumstances. We must never lie to ourselves. If it is true that we do not know perfectly until we love perfectly, it is also true that we do not love perfectly until we know perfectly. A sense of shame holds us back. We feel that we would be giving ourselves away, would be disclosing our own disastrous inadequacy, would be betraying ourselves, but such feelings are out of place in true love, which to the conventional will appear strange, peculiar, exacting, hard at times to recognize as love. It is no use to feel awkward or constrained. So long as that feeling is there, one is not quite oneself. A friend's view is not a critical or a hostile judgment. The things we suffer from lose their power when once they are given utterance. So long as we do not get at the truth, we will lose ourselves in the outer and lie empty within. To surrender our vanity and love of ourselves and expose the naked ribs of reality may mean anguish and sacrifice but it is worth it.[1] Truth, according to the *Mahābhārata*, is penance and sacrifice of a high order. It says: "Truth is always natural with the good. Truth is eternal duty. One should reverentially bow unto truth. Truth is the highest refuge. Truth is duty, truth is penance, truth is yoga. Truth

[1] Cf. Proverbs: "He that covereth his sin shall not prosper; but whoso confesseth and forsaketh them shall have mercy."

is the eternal Brahman. Truth is said to be—sacrifice of a high order. Everything rests on Truth."[1] Truth and reality, not falsehood and semblance are the foundations of lasting friendship, of spiritual life. These friendly revelations have little in common with the exhibitions of spiritual nudism where the sinner speaks exultingly of the depths of sin from which he has emerged to emphasize the heights to which he has attained.

It is the good fortune of some to get the confidence of a few of the unhappy men, the lonely ones, the misfits, who are found in abundance in this world. Those persecuted by society, those reeds shaken by the wind are more appealing than the successful, for we see in them the mystery, the beauty, and the sadness of life. Though there is no special virtue in the hopeless and the outcast, we see in them the struggle of the unconquerable spirit of man with fate or circumstance. The spirit is never broken, however much it may be bent or beaten. We do not know what confidence is, where it comes from, the head or the heart, through what channels it communicates with others. We do not know whether it is visible in the eye or audible in the spoken word. It cannot be acquired through much study and thought. It is a magic gift granted to one and denied to another.

[1] Satyam satsu sadā dharmaḥ satyam dharmah sanātanah
Satyameva namasyeta satyam hi paramā gatih/
Satyam dharmas tapo yogah, satyam brahma sanātanam
Satyam yajñaḥ paraḥ proktaḥ sarvam satye pratiṣṭhitam//
Mahabhārata Sāntiparva, clxii. 4 & 5.

I soon discovered that a small particle of this invaluable gift had been granted to me through no merit of mine. There is a queer impression that Hindus, especially those who talk about philosophy, are more domesticated in the world of spirit. Thanks to it, my correspondence includes letters asking advice and help in every conceivable perplexity. Some of these letters are absurd, some pathetic, and some both. Cranks and faddists fond of their own remedies for the ills of this world are a good many of these correspondents. But now and again one chances on long letters from some old friends, others who through communications have come near, still others who are complete strangers, about their own travails or those of their friends. My relations have little to do with distinctions of age, class or calling, rank or education. It pleases me to know that to some lonely or enslaved souls I was perhaps the only or the first person to show any sympathy or understanding. At times my interest in other people has been so strong and spontaneous that it was misunderstood. There have been cases where the results I expected never arose in spite of my best endeavours. They only indicate that I have not been able to handle these problems with either wisdom or adequacy.

Yet withal, I am happy that I have been brought into human contact with quite a number of my fellow men. I do not believe that there is any such thing as chance or mere coincidence. Desires work unseen through forces of nature. Apparently unimportant happenings sometimes play an unexpected part in our lives. There is such a thing as spiritual gravitation. We can never wholly tell as to why certain people attract us. We cannot help responding to them and finding them interesting. Beauty can never understand itself, says Goethe. Attraction also is only partly explained. Certain persons attach with devotion and why they do so cannot be accounted for. The real causes of our likes and dislikes are usually hidden deep down in the obscure recesses of our nature. They have little to do with reason or logic and we cannot account for them. Wonderful have been the experiences vouchsafed me in this life. Through them the deeps of my own nature have been opened to me in a surprising manner. Through them my life has become more intimately connected with the surrounding social order, more complicated, more difficult and yet far richer and fuller. They have forged links of human affection and regard, given me high joys as well as deep sorrows, and have become inextricably interwoven with the fabric of my life. They in a sense made for genuine fulfilment of destiny.

I have had my own share of anxiety, trouble, and sorrow, but I have had blessings, too, more than I deserve, the chief being the affection and kindness which I receive in abundance from other people. For all these a thankoffering is due. Truly religious souls from Buddha and Christ down to lesser mortals, in spite of gross defects of nature, of mind and heart, have striven to lighten the load of humanity, to strengthen the hopes without which it would have fainted and fallen in its difficult journey. If we are to imitate in some small measure their example, we must help the weak and comfort the unhappy. The perception that casts a shadow over one's existence is that one is not able to take a larger share of the burden of pain that lies upon the world, with its poor and lowly, with its meek and suffering. It does not matter if one has to live one's days in silence, if only it is given in them to smile at a child sometimes, to comfort another human soul in a way that will cheer him and put new hope into his heart.[1]

[1] Na tvaham kāmaye rājyam na svargam nāpunarbhavam/
Kāmaye duḥkhataptānām prāṇinām ārtināśanam//
Bhāgavata ix. 21, 12.

7/11/1934.

BIBLIOGRAPHY

The Philosophy of Rabindranath Tagore. Macmillan, London. Second Impression. 1918.

The Reign of Religion in Contemporary Philosophy. Macmillan, London. 1920.

Indian Philosophy in the Library of Philosophy. Two Volumes. George Allen & Unwin, London. 1923. Revised Second Edition. 1932.

The Hindu View of Life. George Allen & Unwin, London. 1927. Fourth Impression. 1936.

The Religion We Need. Benn. 1928.

Kalki, or The Future of Civilisation. Kegan Paul, London. 1929. Second Impression. 1934.

An Idealist View of Life. George Allen & Unwin, London. 1932. Second Edition. 1937.

East and West in Religion. George Allen & Unwin, London. 1933.

The Heart of Hindusthan. Second Impression. 1932.

Freedom and Culture. 1936. Natesan & Co.

The World's Unborn Soul. Clarendon Press. 1936.

A Pilgrim's Progress

by

C. F. ANDREWS

I

MY mother was by far the most potent influence in my religious life when I was a child. Her love was the one pre-eminent factor in my infancy and early boyhood. It was not so much what she said, or even what she did for me, but rather what she was.

There were Scotch ancestors on my mother's side, though she came directly from a Wessex family with the surname Cartwright. The Highland blood had mingled with the Saxon, and this gave her a mystical vein of character which could be recognized in her face and in her eyes.

The place where I was born was Newcastle-on-Tyne in the north of England. The year of my birth was 1871, and the date February 12th. But when I was still a child my father moved to the Midlands, and I was educated at King Edward VI School, Birmingham, and then on to Cambridge in the year 1890.

When I was between four and five years old, a very severe attack of rheumatic fever nearly proved fatal. For many months my life was almost despaired of and the suffering was very great. But this long illness drew me to my mother with an intense affection, for she nursed me in my pain with a tenderness that created a new bond of affection between us.

My first conscious thoughts about God and Christ were implanted in me at this time by my mother, for I was very close to death, and she used to tell me of the love of Christ for little children and how He took them in His arms and blessed them.

There was a picture of Jesus, the Good Shepherd, which had a great attraction for me. The face of Jesus in the picture used to look at me with the same look of love which I could see in my mother's eyes.

One incident I have told at length in a book called *What I owe to Christ*. It has always clung to my mind during the many years that have passed since it occurred.

For a long time my spirit had been hovering between life and death. Then, one morning, when I opened my eyes, I saw a flower which my mother had put by my bedside while I was asleep. Its fresh beauty seemed to revive me and bring back an interest in life again. From that day recovery was rapid.

The loving care and forethought of my mother had placed that flower beside me, and her unceasing prayers to God had been answered in that way. For He, by whom the very hairs of our head are all numbered and who cares for the fall of a sparrow, had used that tiny event in His good providence to bring me back to health and strength.

It was this illness in childhood that first brought me

into touch with the world of spirit, while I hovered near the border of the unseen and almost passed to the other side. There has often come to me a wonder, why, amid all the changes in my inner thinking, the one fundamental faith in God and Christ and immortality has ever remained unshaken. Surely, my mother's silent influence over me, at such an impressionable age, during the climax of this long illness, must have had very much to do with this.

We are learning to-day from modern psychical investigation what a paramount part is played in our own lives by some shock, or deep impression, left upon the minds in childhood, before we reach the age of five or six. This great shock of illness, with its climax, may have aroused in me a new spiritual sensitiveness which was steeped in emotion owing to the love my mother poured out upon me. Thus, the imagination fixed the record, as it were, on the sensitive plate of my inner mind at a very early age, and it has remained there ever since. What a mother is able to do in this way by her love and her prayers can hardly be exaggerated.

II

My father came from an old East Anglian stock in the county of Essex. He was short in stature and brimming over with vitality. The whole family to which he belonged lived to a good old age. My mother's family was long-lived also.

The long line of ancestors from which my father

was descended were hardy Puritans, who had often endured persecution for conscience' sake. Some had left home and all that they held dear in order to maintain their religious freedom. Men and women, such as these, had sought across the sea in North America a religious liberty which they could not find in England.

While my father had a passionate love of freedom very deeply implanted in him, this did not, in his case, lead on to a hardness and severity of character associated with a Puritan faith. For he was the tenderest of men, and a lover of little children. His Christian faith seemed to reveal itself in an unworldly character, which made him an idealist—generous to the last degree.

When my father was a child his own father, who was a Baptist minister in Essex, had left his congregation to follow certain saintly men who had received, as they believed, wonderful gifts of the Spirit through the ministry of a Scotch Presbyterian minister, named Edward Irving. This young preacher had shaken London society by his sermons upon the Book of Revelation. He declared that the last days of human history had arrived after the downfall of Napoleon. Out of the movement which had thus originated, apostolic gifts of healing and speaking with tongues and prophesying were declared to have been restored to the Christian Church.

As he grew up to manhood, my father himself became a fervent believer. He was quite convinced that he had found the key to the prophetic books in

Holy Scripture and could read the "signs of the times." He himself spoke in prophecy, under the guidance of the Holy Spirit; he had also laid hands on the sick and they had recovered. Therefore he was as certain of the truth of the doctrines which he had learnt to believe as he was of his own existence.

III

It was in this strange, emotional atmosphere of prophesying and speaking with tongues and ecstasy in the Spirit that my own boyhood was passed. Every chapter in the Book of Revelation was explained to me as certain to come to pass in our own days. The solemnity of the religious services was awe-inspiring for a young child, and sometimes the awe was so overwhelming that it brought with it nervous reactions. The Second Coming of the Lord was daily expected. Christ was immediately coming "as a thief in the night" to take away His elect. This phrase, "The Second Coming," was continually upon my father's lips and he lived in expectation of the Advent.

At first my own appreciation of these things which my father taught me was vivid and strong. I had a keenly sensitive imagination, as a boy, and the imagery of the Book of Revelation used to haunt me. But an evil form of impurity crept into my life while I was at school, and gradually I fell away from this earlier belief which had filled my boyhood with awe and wonder.

In the midst of this decline, the inner consciousness of sin made me painfully aware that I was not ready to meet Christ at His Second Coming, if He should suddenly appear. Outwardly, I was leading a strictly religious life, in the bosom of our family, going regularly with my father and mother to church; but inwardly a conflict was going on deep down in the subconscious part of my being, and for a long time this remained unresolved.

Then came a wonderful conversion of my heart to God at the age of nineteen, when I was just about to enter college at Cambridge. So wonderful was it that it changed my whole inner life and released me from the bondage of sin which had bound me fast. Let me tell here very briefly what happened; for it was the great turning-point of my life.

One night the burden of the extreme evil of what I was doing came quite unexpectedly upon me as I knelt down at my bedside to say my prayers. For long hours of darkness I cried out in the agony of my spirit. Then, out of my utter need and helplessness, came a marvellous sense of pardon and release. From that moment the new life in Christ began, which was veritably a new birth. His grace and love flooded my whole being.

The days that followed were like a glorious dream. I seemed to be living in a different world of light and love and peace. It illuminated the glory of Nature, and made me love every one I met.

The effect of this inflow of the Spirit, which came

E

from Christ, was immediately to send me among the poor. Though, up to that time, I was quite unacquainted with that work of service in Christ's name, an inner compulsion seemed to drive me towards it; and all through my life the impulse to surrender all for Christ's sake and to find Him among those who are in need has been present with me so strongly that sooner or later everything has had to give way before it. Although I have never been able literally to obey Christ's command, as St. Francis did, I can well understand the joy which he and his young followers felt in their first love for their Lord and Master, Jesus Christ, when they left all that they had to follow Him. For the happiest moments I have known have always been those when I have been able to find my active work, not in university centres, or among the rich, or even among the middle classes, but among the suffering poor. To say this is not to value lightly those other aspects of human society which I have mentioned, but rather to state a fact in my own individual life which has been verified again and again. For Christ's presence has drawn me towards those who are down-trodden and oppressed; and among these I have found all my love for Him grow deeper.

IV

When I first entered Pembroke College, Cambridge, soon after my conversion, a whole new world of intellectual thought was spread out before me.

Cambridge, towards the end of last century, had reached a unique place of eminence in the sphere of science. The greatness of Darwin and his successors made this recognized in every sphere.

At first it was quite natural for me to find my companions among those who knew the joy of complete surrender to Christ, and regarded His Second Coming as at hand, just as I had been taught to regard it. These friends I found among the fundamentalists, who believed in the verbal inspiration of Holy Scripture. But I soon found myself turning away in revolt, because they held a monstrous doctrine of everlasting punishment for the mass of the human race. This doctrine my father had always condemned as inconsistent with God's name of Love. Later on, I was compelled by sheer honesty to accept the facts of modern scientific discovery. The increasing knowledge of God's universe soon made verbal inspiration of Holy Scripture impossible to hold as a living faith. To Cambridge, more than any other place in the world, I owe the code of intellectual honour (if I may call it by that name) which ought always to go side by side with a true faith in Christ, as the Lord of Truth. Only thus could I fulfil the word of the Apostle who said: "Prove all things; hold fast that which is good."

From all this it followed that very soon I found my father's interpretations of the prophetic books of the Bible to be in conflict with the scientific explanation of world history and its results. The conviction on this point was naturally far longer in coming home to me than my judgment on other points which I have mentioned above. But when it did come at last, and I had to face it, then immediately I wrote home to my father a letter which very deeply pained him. As soon as I met him in the vacation, we argued the matter out together, while misunderstanding between us only deepened.

Then followed one of the greatest struggles of my life. For I had been told by the doctor that my father was suffering from an acute form of heart disease which might at any moment prove fatal. The order, therefore, had been given that he must be kept entirely free from nervous excitement of any kind.

Already I had witnessed the agony from which he suffered during one of the worst paroxysms of heart-attack, and I had also watched the agony on my mother's face as she tended to him in his pain. In my intense affection, I could not bear to run the risk of bringing on the nervous excitement which was certain to happen if I carried my own argument to this extreme point. So I said to myself, "No, I cannot go on with this any longer. I *must* not speak any more about it while my father is in this critical state. If I do so, I may be responsible for his death!"

For this reason I continually compromised, though my conscience pricked me all the while. Again and again I prayed that this burden might be taken from me; and I tried by going to others, who held the same faith as my father, to get an answer from them which would satisfy my doubtings. How I longed to be convinced that my father was right, but that was impossible. For the mind's verdict became inexorably clear that I could no longer hold these peculiar beliefs and at the same time accept everything that modern research was making plain to the human mind.

For some years, until 1895, I went on still attending the church in Birmingham, where my father was beloved by the whole congregation. During the service, I would try to enter into the spirit of what was said and sung, but more and more the worshippers appeared to me to be living in a different world of thought from my own. Yet I went on attending, for my father's and mother's sake, long after I had ceased to hold their own particular faith.

From this perilous position, which was already bordering on deceit, I was rescued by the forceful action of Basil Westcott. He was the youngest son of the saintly Bishop of Durham, Dr. Westcott, the New Testament scholar and professor. Basil was my dearest college friend, whose love for me was too deep to allow me to continue this weakening compromise any longer. I told him everything and introduced him to my father and mother. He knew from me the whole situation. But he was brave enough to tell me that our friendship must be broken unless I was prepared to be more honest with myself and both my parents. He told me also to leave the question of my father's health in God's hands.

Then at last I faced the whole situation and after a time of incredible pain gave up openly my father's beliefs and left the Church which had been hitherto my spiritual home.

The actual break came when I was confirmed in Lichfield Cathedral and ceased from that time forward to receive the Holy Communion at my father's hands, as I had done before.

This incident I have told here at length, because my whole future course depended upon it. Looking back, there can be no doubt in my mind that it was right to take the step I did, in an honest and truthful manner. But I have often wondered since whether my break with my father's faith need have been so complete, when our underlying devotion to our Lord Jesus Christ was the same. It is hard for me to-day to think that Christ's own Sacrament of Unity should have become an open barrier between myself and those whom I loved best in the world.

But in those days it seemed right to all of us that I should take this course. At that time of my life I used to lay a primary stress on High Church doctrines. This would be impossible for me to-day. The Church wherein my father was a minister was "high" both in its ritual and teaching. The Holy Eucharist was celebrated with vestments and incense, and the Sacrament was reserved as in the Roman and Greek Churches. My friend Basil Westcott was an Anglo-Catholic, and I was much influenced by his religious views, as this story of mine will have made plain. Through his invalid sister, also, who was never able to leave her sick-room, I had begun to realize with deep reverence the "beauty of holiness." Therefore all my traditions hitherto had gone in the High Church direction. Ecclesiastical questions loomed very large in my mind.

Yet, all the while, far beyond any outward allegiances, there was now growing up day by day an inner allegiance to Christ Himself, which made me long to follow Him more faithfully and truly in my own personal life. In the silent devotions, at the daily Eucharist, I would renew my tryst; and that quiet time in the early morning became very precious to me. But above all, whenever I got away from Cambridge University and came into close personal contact with those whom Christ specially loved— the poor, the sick, the suffering—the love in my heart for my Lord blossomed out into flower. The intellectual questionings themselves became less acute, and I realized how far beyond abstract logic lay the great moral factors of our existence.

Probably, if I had married during these years of moral and spiritual stress, and had a home of my own, with little children to teach me to be humble and gentle, the great central truths of the Christian faith would have become more real and vital to me. But the intense desire, which was gradually forming in my own mind, to go out to the mission field and join the Cambridge University Brotherhood at Delhi, prevented me from ever contemplating such an action, for only unmarried men are accepted into that Brotherhood.

After a long university course at Cambridge had been completed, I was ordained in 1896 to the Pembroke College Mission, in Walworth, which is one of the poorest parts of South-East London. There some of the happiest years of my life were spent among the poor. The joy of Christ's own service of love was so great that no labour seemed too hard for me at that time.

But after some years, while actively engaged in this work, I overstrained myself and was obliged in the end, under doctor's orders, to surrender it. An invitation to go back as a teacher to Cambridge came at this critical juncture, and I was induced to accept it. There, too, in the University, years of great happiness were spent, mingled with great sorrows. For I came face to face with death, among those I loved most dearly, not once only but again and again. During those solemn days, when death was my constant companion, the Christian faith became rooted and grounded in me with a new intensity of conviction. I seemed to be continually living with Christ on the very border of the unseen world.

Yet in spite of great inward happiness and renewed spiritual vision, which followed my ordination, the difficulties which I had to face in my own intellectual life did not seem to decrease. New questionings arose. The recitation, in a Christian act of worship, of the

imprecatory Psalms, calling down vengeance on
enemies, who were not only hated, but cursed, became
almost intolerable to me. The Athanasian Creed
with its damnatory clauses was an even greater stumb-
ling block. The Thirty-nine Articles, to which I had
subscribed, began also to trouble me; and however
much I might try to ease my conscience by regarding
mere assent to them as allowing latitude of acceptance,
it was difficult to be quite clear in my own mind that
I was not again deceiving myself just as I had done
before.

Although I was still a long way off from coming
to conclusions on these and other matters, I began
more and more to realize that the only solution of
all my intellectual troubles was to get back to the
simplicity of the Gospel in my daily life. This was my
one dominating thought during my second period
at Cambridge as a teacher, and in my heart I knew
that I must be ready to follow Christ still more
completely and not shrink from any sacrifice which
He called upon me to make in His name.

V

The call came at last in a very sudden and tragic
manner. My friend Basil Westcott died at Delhi
of cholera, while trying to save the life of another.
His death made a very deep impression on me, and I
sailed for India as soon as ever I could be set free to
do so, in order to take his place.

But in India still more fundamental problems of the mind came before me for solution. The Virgin Birth of Christ, as a literal and historical fact, and also the resurrection of Christ's body from the grave, had long ago become matters of doubt and questioning to me on the historical side, and I had studied every scrap of evidence concerning them. In the end I had decided to suspend my judgment. Neither of these matters vitally affected my faith in the living Christ, who was present with me in my daily life.

But it was one thing to hold these matters in suspense for a while in England; it was quite a different thing being called upon to teach them in a new country, such as India, where a young Church was beginning to spring up. The words of Jesus about causing the "little ones" to stumble made me feel the deep responsibility for what I was doing.

Of the supernatural character of our Lord's work of ministry on earth and His risen life beyond the grave, I rarely had any question. He was, and is, to me the Living Christ, to whom I have continually looked for spiritual sustenance and renewal. He is the daily Companion of the pilgrim journey I have undertaken in His strength.

While, therefore, at first in Delhi it did not seem necessary for me to come to a final decision about all these matters, yet in the end the whole issue of what, in the Church of England, is called "subscription" was forced upon me.

VI

The joy came into my life, at this time, of a great transforming friendship with Susil Kumar Rudra, the principal of my own college. He used to go, each year, up into the mountains with me, beyond Simla. His two sons used to accompany us and sometimes students from college were with us also. Susil had lost his wife, owing to an illness after the birth of his youngest child, and he had never married again.

There, at Kotgarh, we met Samuel Stokes of Germanstown, Philadelphia, who was living a Franciscan life along with Sadhu Sundar Singh. About the Sadhu I have written very fully in a memoir which has been published in America and England. He is also referred to in other books which I have written. His love for Christ was so ardent that my own love was kindled by it. I found in him, also, one who had not ceased to reverence that which was pure and noble and of good report in his old religious faith. He felt that he had received the consummation of it all in his Lord and Master, Jesus Christ.

It was in this atmosphere of the glorious mountains, with their snows reaching up into the blue sky, that the narrowness of the boundaries of my former religious faith was made clear to me, and the decision was slowly formed within me to seek a wider sphere of work.

The break actually came when, in 1913, I was asked by Mr. Gokhale to go out to South Africa in order to help in the Indian cause at a time of great anxiety and danger.

A form of servile labour called "indenture" had been in operation for many years. Villagers from India had been induced to leave India and go out to the sugar-plantations. The whole system of recruiting was corrupt beyond description.

The moral conditions on these plantations were deplorable. Mahatma Gandhi had started a passive resistance movement in order to bring to an end, once and for all, these widespread evils.

He had suffered imprisonment with more than two thousand of his followers and the struggle had reached a very critical point. General Smuts represented the South African Government.

It was in order to help in this passive resistance struggle that Mr. Gokhale invited me to go out to Natal. Willie Pearson, the son of the great Congregational minister of Manchester, Dr. Samuel Pearson, went with me. In the end the passive resistance struggle was won and Mahatma Gandhi was able to return to India.

But the vicious system of Indian indenture still existed in other parts of the world, such as Fiji, Trinidad, British Guiana, etc. In order to obtain its abolition, further journeys were necessary and I had to go twice to Fiji.

At last, in 1920, this form of Indian indentured labour was altogether abolished. The day, January 1st, will go down in Indian history as parallel to the date on which slavery was abolished in the British dominions and later on in the United States. Now, in India, all recruiting for such a purpose abroad has been entirely prohibited.

This experience in South Africa and elsewhere widened my outlook upon life and gave me a new world vision of the Christian faith. When I went back to India from South Africa, it soon became clear to me that I could no longer remain in the more confined sphere of the Cambridge Brotherhood at Delhi. With the kindliest recognition of the larger field of work which had opened out for me, the Head of the Mission, the Rev. Canon Allnutt, bade me God speed, and allowed me to depart.

But something still further happened almost at the same time, though I had not expected it to come about in this way. All these earlier questionings about subscription to the Prayer-book and Thirty-nine Articles now came to a head; and at last it was clear to me that I ought no longer to exercise my full Orders in the Anglican ministry under a bishop's licence.

What heart-searching I went through before the final step was taken I have told in *What I owe to Christ*.[1] It was like tearing up very deep roots and transplanting the whole of my religious life into a new soil.

The incident which made it impossible for me to go on any longer in doubt and vacillation is worth

[1] Published by the Abingdon Press, New York, and Hodder & Stoughton, London.

recalling. Rabindranath Tagore had invited me to join his institution at Santiniketan. In his magnanimity he had agreed to take me just as I was, an ordained clergyman. He wished me to continue all my religious duties as far as possible, while at the same time working with him, at Santiniketan, in his great educational work.

But when Trinity Sunday came and I was faced with the recital of the Athanasian Creed, I suddenly found that I could not repeat it, with its damnatory clauses. It came home to me with a shock that I could not lead an Indian Christian congregation in the recitation of that Creed and then go back light-heartedly to Santiniketan as if nothing had happened. So I omitted the Creed altogether. But at once I recognized that I was playing a coward's part in thus trifling with my conscience.

When I returned and saw the pure face of the poet Rabindranath looking into my own, I knew at once that I had been living a life of untruth. So there and then I confessed to him with shame all that had happened and how from henceforth I must be truthful.

He urged me earnestly to take no hasty step. But when I showed him how near to the brink of the precipice of falsehood I had been, he said no more to dissuade me.

Thus, the inner struggle, that had gone on for so many years, had suddenly come to an end.[1] But bitter

[1] *What I owe to Christ*, chapter xvi.

wounds had been left behind which took many years to heal.

Nevertheless, it soon became clear that this action meant to me not only a release from bondage, but also a greater power of Christian service. The blessing of God had been with me, leading me forward.

Since that step was taken I have gradually come to recognize that Christ Himself in His Gospel has given us His own definition of discipleship and also of membership in His Body, which is called the Household of faith. For He has said plainly: "He that doeth the will of God, the same is my brother and my sister and my mother."

If this is Christ's own definition it is not for us to draw boundaries more narrowly than our Lord Himself had drawn them. Where this will lead me ultimately is not yet clear. But it will certainly make a vast difference in my own conception of what a Christian is and what he ought to be.

VII

Two special errors, on a large scale, in my own way of thinking, concerning India became apparent to me when I came into touch with reality at first hand by living among Indians themselves.

On one side, to apply the Golden Rule of Christ to the British occupation of India was by no means such a simple thing as I had before imagined. It was made evident to me, by abundant examples, that the great historian, Sir J. R. Seeley, was right when he wrote long ago in his *Expansion of England*: "Subjection for a long time to a foreign yoke is one of the most potent causes of national deterioration."

While it might be true that the early effects of the occupation of India by Great Britain had been to bring about a nation-wide awakening, it now was equally clear to me that to continue to rule India from without by foreign rule must lead on, as Seeley has told us, to national deterioration.

Would I wish my own country to continue for a long time in subjection to a foreign yoke? If I would *not* wish this, then what right had I to continue to take part in imposing this very thing on India?

Convictions like these, slowly formed, made me one of the whole-hearted workers for Indian freedom and independence.

But the problem was not so easy, even then. How was Indian freedom to be won, without an interval of chaos and confusion? The government could not be merely handed back to the Indian people by Great Britain, after more than a century of disuse on their part, making them weaker and weaker. That might mean only a new bondage. What was clearly needed was a dynamic personality in India itself, who could bring a new freedom about from within—not by violence, but by self-sacrifice. For this would create the very spirit of true libety and independence which was essentially needed.

This dynamic quality I found in the two friends

who gradually became the formative influences in my thinking life—the poet Rabindranath Tagore, and Mahatma Gandhi. These two have brought to me quite unconsciously, but very intimately, a fuller interpretation of what the message of Christ actually means in the modern world. In the great struggle for Indian freedom their voices have been prophetic, and Mahatma Gandhi, by his living example, made known in deeds which the simplest villager can understand, has been able to create among the Indian masses the true spirit of freedom which was needed.

This leads me directly to the second point where I had to correct many of my previous ideas.

While I had never consciously held the narrow view that the rest of God's world, outside the boundaries of Christendom, was lying in "heathen darkness," I had not at all realized before the beauty of the lives of those in India and other countries who had been true seekers after God. They had followed other pathways of the religious life, but had in the end found Him whom their souls desired. For Christ Himself had said: "Seek, and ye shall find; knock, and it shall be opened to you."

Before my new experience in India, I had taken this gracious promise, unthinkingly, as concerned only with those who were Christian and had not realized how in its widest sense it is an invitation to all mankind.

With this new vision I began to see Christ in these saintly men and women whom I met both in Islam and in the Hindu religion. It was quite natural to me

F

to speak to them of what I owed to Christ and to share my own religious experiences with them. This was done, however, not as to those who required first of all to be enlightened by me, but rather as to those who had themselves a background of spiritual conviction, about which I longed to hear. Mere proselytizing, which Christ Himself clearly abhorred,[1] went out of my mind, and what in the Oxford Group Movement is called "sharing" took its place.

Thus, in both these aspects, the old "imperialist" outlook, whether political or religious, became abhorrent to me, and I was able to understand what wrong had been done to India by this attitude of superiority. It became more and more a necessity of my Christian faith to get rid of every trace of this evil from my own heart.

The words of Christ recorded in St. Luke's Gospel were filled with a new meaning, as I faced this great world issue. "The Kings of the Gentiles," says Christ, "exercise lordship over them, and they that exercise authority upon them are called Benefactors, but it shall not be so with you. But he that is greatest among you let him be as the younger, and he that is chief as he that doth serve. For whether is greater, he that sitteth at meat, or he that serveth? Is not he that sitteth at meat? But I am among you as he that serveth."

Another line of development for me at this time was to take to heart, in practical life, as well as in

[1] See Matthew xxiii. 15.

theory, the magnificently triumphant words of St. Paul concerning Christ: "There is neither Jew nor Greek, there is neither bond nor free, there is neither male nor female: for ye are all one Man in Christ Jesus." And again he writes in the same strain, "Where there is neither Greek nor Jew, circumcision nor uncircumcision, barbarian, Scythian, bond nor free, but Christ is all and in all."

This determination to break down every "middle wall of partition" between man and man, which racial and colour prejudice had caused, became henceforth a burning passion. It is still, to-day, at the centre of all my thoughts and actions.

VIII

During all these new experiences of the larger issues of human life, Dr. Albert Schweitzer's book *The Quest of the Historical Jesus* came to me with a refreshing shock and cleared away a mass of confused thinking. I shall never forget the challenge that this volume brought with it. By the very opposition with which I at first received his main thesis I was inwardly conscious of the truth which lay behind it. Coming back to it to-day it is easy to see that the stress he has laid upon eschatology in Christ's teaching is one-sided. But it was necessary thus to redress the balance, which had swung in the opposite direction.

In my own case, the book revealed to me how I had been drifting towards a complacent and patronizing "humanist" attitude, and had left out of count the startlingly supernatural claim to absolute allegiance which Christ makes. Schweitzer's last chapter brought me sharply back to reality. It made me renew, with a fresh conviction, my faith in a supernatural Christ who commands by His moral grandeur.

Furthermore, Schweitzer's whole thesis made me go back again to the days of my early childhood so as to recall my father and mother's daily expectation of Christ's coming. I could see now that this ardent "prevision" of crisis, this sense of impending judgment, had to be maintained if the Christian faith of our own day was to be true to type. But at the same time, this expectation had to be taken out of its local setting and viewed in the light of the Eternal.

Thus, I have tried to explain what Schweitzer's book in a very searching manner effected for me. Are we ready, he asks, to take Christ literally, honestly, sincerely, as our own life-guide? Are we prepared to leave all and follow Him, just as Peter and James and John were? For Christ must not be for us a mere figure in past history, but our Lord and Master, commanding our soul's allegiance.

"Christ comes to us," writes Schweitzer, "as One Unknown, without a name, just as of old by the lake-side He came to those men who knew Him not. He speaks to us in the same words, 'Follow thou Me,' and sets us to those tasks which He has to fulfil for our time. He commands. And to those who obey Him, whether they be wise or simple, He will reveal

Himself in the toils, the conflicts, the sufferings which they shall pass through in His fellowship. And as an ineffable mystery they shall learn in their own experience who He is."

The greatest of all influences which Albert Schweitzer has had on my own life has been due to the example of his own devotion. For he had literally left all to follow Christ and had dedicated all that he had to the service of the sick and dying, in the name of Christ, living in a malarial belt in tropical Africa, at Lambarene. His own example has thus driven me back to those crucial sufferings among the poor, to those homes of the meek and lowly, to the lives of those who labour and are heavy-laden, which have always drawn me most of all with the cords of love and led me back to Christ.

In later years, Albert Schweitzer has become known to me, not merely through his books, but personally as an intimate friend. He has shown me in personal ways the truth of the great word in St. John's Gospel, "If any man will do His will, he shall know the doctrine whether it be of God."

IX

The Great War brought to light a tragic hesitation within me to apply fearlessly and immediately the principles of Christ to war. On this lack of insight I now must look back with shame. For when my own country was involved I found myself wavering and doubtful, torn with questionings which could not be resolved.

The brutality and cruelty, the meanness and false-hood of war soon brought with them moral shocks, which ought to have aroused me to action. Yet instead of this, the war-spirit found a lodgment in my own mind, and I could almost feel rising within a secret eagerness for a victory for my country, at whatever moral cost.

Yet when this appeared on the surface I despised myself for it and was horrified to find what a hold it had got over me. The scales at last fell from my eyes and I saw war as the hateful thing it was—clean contrary to the Golden Rule of Christ. Then at last, when the question of military conscription in India was brought up before me as a practical issue, my mind was fully prepared and I refused.

I did not have to suffer for this refusal, but was ready to do so and had counted the cost. During this terrible crisis and inner suffering Christ Himself became inexpressibly dear to me. Just as I had found Him among the poor, in the slums of Walworth, so I found Him near to me when this great trial of faith came. For I had to learn, in singular ways, what perse-cution means, and His own blessing, which He has promised to those who suffer with Him, filled my heart with joy.

All this was far beyond any deserving; for like Peter I had at first denied my Lord. But He had accepted my contrition, and healed me with His own forgiveness. After that He had given to me once more His own command, "Follow Me."

X

Though much remains to be told, this story of my life must now be brought to a close. I can only very briefly refer to one further direction in which my thoughts to-day are tending.

The issue between Capital and Labour in its modern form has lately occupied my thoughts night and day. My friend, Sherwood Eddy, has done much to make me face it as a Christian. The vast injustice of an order of society which allows one man to amass incredible wealth while others are starving needs no long argument to prove how contrary to the mind of Christ it is. Like slavery and war, the system of unrestricted capitalism, in its present form, is one of those giant evil forces of the world, creating selfishness and greed, which the Christian conscience must condemn. Our Lord Jesus Christ spoke words of sternness against those who heaped up riches while their brothers went hungry and naked. His judgment on such is unqualified in its condemnation. It is quite impossible for any one to say that these social wrongs are outside the limits of the Christian message, for Christ Himself has no words strong enough to utter against the motives of greed which form the basis of the present evil world.

But how to change human society from within, so

that capitalism, with its money-greed, becomes a hateful thing to a Christian, just as usury was in the Middle Ages, and slavery was in the nineteenth century, and war is becoming to-day! This is perhaps the greatest of all questions that the Christian who follows Christ has to face and answer in our own age.

There are methods of violence and class warfare whereby the end in view may be forcibly attempted. But history shows clearly that such a use of violence brings its own nemesis with it. "They that take the sword," says Christ, "shall perish with the sword." For this reason, as a Christian, I feel that I can no more join in a war to abolish Capital than I can join in a war to abolish war itself.

Yet I am convinced that there are means, not of violence, but of non-violence, whereby a new social order, more in accord with the mind of Christ, may be ushered into our modern world, making it indeed a "new earth." India has much to teach Europe and America concerning these things, if only the West will have humility and patience enough to learn the lesson from her. In my own life I can say with deep conviction that I have learnt more about Christ's Cross of suffering during the years of my life spent in the East than I was able to do while I lived in Europe. For it has slowly, but marvellously, become clear to me that there are vast reserves of spiritual power for good stored up by Divine Providence in human hearts, which can be used, if rightly directed, in overcoming evil. These resources are abundant in the East.

But only as we cease to rely upon those material weapons which to-day in the West appear to be all-powerful, can these almighty forces of the Spirit of the Living God be set free. When once the day of faith dawns, the victory is certain. For the paradox is true, that only as man feels his own weakness does he realize the almighty strength of God, and only as he loses his life can he save it.[1]

PRINCIPAL PUBLICATIONS

Christ and Labour. S.C.M. Press, London.

Mahatma Gandhi's Ideas. George Allen & Unwin, London.

Mahatma Gandhi—His Own Story. George Allen & Unwin, London.

Mahatma Gandhi at Work. George Allen & Unwin, London.

India and the Simon Report. George Allen & Unwin, London.

The Indian Earthquake. George Allen & Unwin, London.

Letters to a Friend (*Tagore*). Edited by C.F.A. George Allen & Unwin, London.

What I Owe to Christ. Hodder & Stoughton, London.

Christ in the Silence. Hodder & Stoughton, London.

Sadhu Sundar Singh. Hodder & Stoughton, London.

John White of Mashonaland. Hodder & Stoughton, London.

Zaka Ullah of Delhi. W. Heffer, Cambridge.

Opium in Assam. S.C.M. Press, London.

Christianity and the Labour Conflict. Methuen, London.

India and Britain—A Moral Challenge. S.C.M. Press, London.

[1] Those who would care to study further what I have thus written in bare outline should read *What I owe to Christ*, published by the Abingdon Press, New York, and Hodder & Stoughton, London.

My Own Little Theatre

by

GEORGE A. COE[1]

Professor of Education (Retired), Teacher's College, Columbia University

BY what route have I arrived at the convictions that I now hold with respect to the major issues of human life? In particular, why have I "changed cars" several times since my journey started? To answer these questions with even approximate fullness one would have to write a biography of the modern type—the type that probes the obscure parts of a personality, and measures the impact upon it of the subtler forces in the environment. My thought-life is to be explained partly by my temperament, and this by my endocrine glands; partly by the forces with which psychoanalysis chiefly deals, for inferiority and superiority complexes, infantile attachments and repulsions, and sex drives and repressions must have coloured my experience, and my experience must have coloured my theories; partly by environmental forces that I did not recognize at the time as the influence of my economic setting in the petty bourgeoisie, and likewise

---

[1] Born at Mendon, Monroe Co., N.Y., March 26, 1862. Academic study: University of Rochester, Boston University School of Theology, University of Berlin. Professorships: University of Southern California (1888–90), North-western University (1891–1909), Union Theological Seminary (1909–22), Teachers' College of Columbia University (1922–7). Retired, 1927.

the influence of the "climate of opinion" in religious and academic circles in which I have moved; partly by contacts with strong personalities, conjugal affection, domestic life, friendship, and gregarious enjoyments; partly, surely, by self-interest, some of it unrecognized as such. If I were to write an autobiography, all these would have to be canvassed.

But this essay is not to be an autobiography. It is to expose only such phases of my thought-life as came rather clearly to the surface. When there was need for planned action, or for meeting other minds in discussion, or for assuaging recognized friction in my beliefs, then things otherwise obscure came to the light, and my thinking became consciously mine. There are inherent satisfactions in such above-board thinking, and of course satisfaction in an activity leads to more activity of the same kind. I judge that the pleasurable thrill of endeavouring to think things through has been mine in a degree that is not less than the average. My endeavour now to recall such parts of my past is accompanied, however, by full realization that it is a characteristic of memory partly to reconstruct what it purports merely to reproduce, and that retrospection inevitably includes interpretation.

The thought-process, where it is most alive, is dramatic. For it is awakened by conflict, or by some other blocking of a mental movement; pits alternatives against one another; includes suspense while the struggle goes on, and only so attains to some degree of relaxation in an at least tentative conclusion.

Thus each of us has a stage of his own, and each of us is at the same time playwright (or co-playwright), stage-manager, audience, dramatic critic, and the "behind the scenes." What I am now endeavouring to recall is the appearance and the dialogue of the actors when they were out before the footlights of my own little theatre. This means that I must trace out a series of problems and conflicts.

Reared in the family of a Methodist minister, I early became familiar with conventional formulas for Christian belief and with conventional practices of piety. I took the validity of the whole for granted, just as I accepted the Constitution of the United States. Though I recall no instance of parental pressure to make me conform, and though my childhood and youth were more than ordinarily free from sense of restraint, nevertheless I was a young Conformist. Not quite a passive one, however, for I began at an early age to take an interest in thought-structures. For example, when a college course in the history of philosophy acquainted me with Aristotle's theory of a "prime mover," I suddenly became aware that this line of reasoning was not new to me, and that I had heard Aristotle's argument when I was seven or eight years old in a sermon on the existence of God preached by the Rev. John Parker.

How, then, did I become a Nonconformist? By no single, climactic, or emotional revolt, but by a series of rather mild episodes. The first of them concerned religious experience. Methodist piety, when I was young, laid great store by "testimony" to a "personal experience" of "conversion" and "witness of the Spirit" or "assurance" that one had been pardoned and "accepted" of God. Inasmuch as I had responded step by step to the rather genial nurture of my home, it was impossible, when I reached adolescence, to recognize myself as a Christian in this, the standard Methodist sense. Too clear-headed either to interpret my past as that of a sinner outside the gate, or to undergo "conversion" in any of the numerous revivals, I suffered a period of stress. Nothing that I could find in my father's library helped. But when I was already more than half-way through my college course I cut the knot by a rational and ethical act. Assuming that my part in the matter was to continue to commit myself to the Christian way of life, and that internal "witness" or "assurance" was not my affair, I resolved that never again would I seek it. This ended the turmoil.

But it did something more than relieve an adolescent's emotional tension. It started a habit of looking for the core of religious experience in the ethical will; moreover, it led on towards endeavours to explain the experiences that some had while I did not have them. Merely to refer them to God as their source explained nothing, and besides it was misleading. In my earliest years as a college teacher I came upon so many cases of this misleading— youths religiously devoted yet in religious darkness —that, as I now see the matter, it became practically inevitable that, sooner or later, I should attempt a psychological study in this field. Owing, however, to the heavy demands of a whole college "settee" of philosophy I was to print little in this or any field until near the close of the nineteenth century.

When, in the nineties, the country was swept by a gust of interest in adolescence, I participated in studies of this period of growth. Characteristically, I made an investigation (a small one) and published an article on "The Morbid Conscience of Adolescents." By this time I was moved in such matters as much, perhaps, by scientific curiosity and the immediate satisfactions of scientific inquiry as by interest in religion; yet it must have been a continuing sense of the importance of religion that caused my curiosity to centre where it did.(15) In 1899 I plunged definitely into psychology of religion with "A Study in the Dynamics of Personal Religion."(11) Shortly afterward this article was included in a little volume, *The Spiritual Life*, which was concerned largely, though not exclusively, with conversion and other experiences that include an automatic factor.(1) Though the methods of research that underlay this volume we now should call crude, they were the best in use at that time in such fields, and they yielded results which, at the most important point, the *dynamics* of the experiences concerned, still appear to be substantially valid.

I have now traced one of my intellectual interests to the beginning of its fruit-bearing. Others were developing at the same period. My mental history resembles a rope in that many filaments that are separable are twisted together. Following one of these filaments "'round and 'round," I have left behind one not less important. For in my adolescence a second episode occurred that has influenced all my mature thinking. It concerned the controversy over evolution. I was born only three years after Darwin published *The Origin of Species.* The furore that it created in Church circles was still hot when, a senior in college, I was introduced to the science of zoology. I was fortunate enough to have a teacher, Harrison E. Webster, who, besides being a competent biologist, was an intellectual inspiration. He led me to realize what the method and the spirit of science are, to read Darwin for myself (both *The Origin of Species* and *The Descent of Man*), and to enjoy the articulation of empirical data. No one needed to tell me how contrary this was to the modes of thought and to some of the conclusions that from childhood I had supposed to be revealed truth. For me an issue was squarely joined. It concerned chiefly the validity of a method. How is the truth to be found in matters of this kind? I settled the question, as far as I was concerned, on a Sunday morning by solemnly espousing the scientific method, including it within my religion, and resolving to follow it wherever it should lead. Of course, I did not then realize what a revolutionary step this was for one reared in a dogmatic Christianity; I merely knew that for me to live either intellectually or spiritually I must follow the scientific gleam.

The next act upon the stage of "my own little theatre" presents a struggle among ideas in a theological seminary. No deep conviction that I was "called" to the ministry set me at the study of theology; rather, I had gravitated in this direction because, as my father's son, I was constantly in touch with Church life and its problems, and had a habit of thinking about them. In spite of the fact that the president of my college, the revered Martin B. Anderson, had predicted that I should become a teacher in the employ of my Church, I expected to become a pastor. But before I had completed my first year at the Boston University School of Theology, three of my professors, each independently of the other two, came to the conclusion that I was "cut out for" a professor, specifically a professor of systematic theology. Accordingly, I was advised to bend my studies in this direction. I did so "with a vengeance," and in addition, under the guidance of President Warren, I read extensively upon the religions of the world, and under the fascination of Professor Bowne I listened, and read, and rejoiced in the field of philosophy.

A second theological interest arose through the teaching of the Old Testament by Professor Hinckley G. Mitchell. The "higher criticism" was then under fire in this country, even in some of the more intelligent Church circles. Though Mitchell's type of criticism was exceedingly mild it was exceedingly honest, and it was courageous. It appealed to me just as Professor Webster's treatment of evolution had done, and for the same reason. For a time reverence for the spirit of science as Webster and Mitchell exemplified it lived in the same young breast with systematic theology. But the incompatibility was bound to come to the surface of my mind. Not only was there a difference in procedure and atmosphere; intensive reading in theology convinced me that it required a metaphysical basis that it did not possess. For this reason—doubtless there were others also—the study of philosophy with Professor Bowne superseded my study of theological systems.

At one point my mind attained clarity at this time. Theology, as it came to me, depended for its validity upon its primary discipline, apologetics; but apologetics took its conclusion for granted from the outset. Considered as a matter of formal logic, then, the theology that I knew was one great *petitio principii* or "begging of the question." There was involved an assumption that there is a kind of authority that can settle details of fact, or of value, or of duty before we have inspected them, whereas the method of the sciences and of historical criticism proceeded in the opposite direction. Before the end of my four years at Boston (I remained a fourth year in order to study philosophy and the religions of the world) I had recognized this incompatibility, and had ceased to aspire to occupy a chair in a theological seminary. Instead, I endeavoured to be a professor of philosophy.

To move out from under a theological roof did not imply, however, rejection of all the doctrines that it housed, much less indifference to the experienced values that were more or less associated with them. These doctrines and values required examination, each by itself. As there could be no wholesale acceptance, so there could be no wholesale rejection. This will explain how I have been able to retain through all the subsequent years a sense of my continuity with historical Christianity. But my rejection of theological orthodoxy on the ground that it depends upon a fallacious view of authority has turned out to be only the beginning of a fruitful experience. For I was to learn that there are many orthodoxies besides the theological ones—political orthodoxies, social orthodoxies, economic orthodoxies, ethical orthodoxies, educational orthodoxies, for example—all of them constituted of individual or collective self-imitation, and all of them resistant to the creativity that is potential in man.(8) I discovered, too, that an authority that is expelled through the door can come back through the window, and that all minds have windows as well as doors.

This door-and-window relationship early revealed itself in the religious thinking that went on about me. Though I no longer imposed upon myself the duty of keeping abreast of theological thought, I could not fail to know that sometimes the freedom that liberal theology practised was freedom to weave merely the fringes of the garment. As time went on, a great hiatus revealed itself. Rigorous research with respect to the biblical literature, but no corresponding rigour with respect to the great issues of life and society that reach all the way from Old Testament times to the present; critical analysis of the Gospels, but uncritical encomiums upon the character of Jesus, and romantic assumptions as to His significance in history or in the cosmos; incisive history of the Church, but, with respect to the Church of to-day, acquiescence upon a basis that is both uncritical of contemporary ecclesiastical facts, and ethically complacent; proclamations that Christianity is a way of life rather than a set of beliefs, but failure to show how it differs from other, contemporary ways of life; a wide orbit in the upper air of concepts, together with unimpeachable sentiments, but here on the ground, enormous ethical conflicts and forces scarcely named in these concepts, and not controlled by these sentiments—all this was to unfold before me, and partly within me. It seems to me now that the liberal evangelicalism with which I have had many contacts has attempted to be religiously orthodox but theologically free. In this there is neither intellectual nor spiritual consistency, and of course there cannot be in it power to guide the course of events even within the Church, to say nothing of society at large.(26)

In the immediately preceding paragraph I have

summarized insights that came to me gradually through a long series of years. Now I must return to my student days in order to inspect the philosophical railroad to which I had switched from the theological. In Borden P. Bowne diverse interests and methods mingled without being able to fuse. He was wholly with Mitchell in the controversy over biblical criticism. In respect to the guidance of the religious life he was pragmatic rather than speculative. Here he spoke a winsome language which, if he had not been a philosopher, might have made him eminent as a religious leader. He even included in his theory of theism an appeal to experienced values as a final ground of belief. But these empirical and valuational attitudes were offset in his metaphysics and theory of knowledge by a speculative process which he called the working over of concepts. This process was inspired and guided by a theological purpose. In some Church circles he was regarded as a radical thinker and dangerous to orthodoxy, but this opinion was superficial. There was, indeed, something of the happy iconoclast in him; he did use a harsh broom upon crude ideas that students brought to the classroom, and he laughed some sorts of ignorant orthodoxy out of court. Yet his own central interest, as he himself realized, was to provide an epistemological and metaphysical basis for the main theses of orthodoxy. His philosophy was in reality theological apologetics, and it harboured in its own way the fallacy of authority that I was learning to reject.

Partly through study in Germany, but more through contacts with thought and research in the United States, I came to the conclusion that even his justified attacks upon Herbert Spencer and upon various kinds of hasty "scientific" philosophizing did not resolve the main difficulty that the scientific movement had created for religious faith. He was right, I then believed and still do believe, in taking the nature of the personal self as the crux of the problem. This "jumped with my humour," moreover, for ever since I chose "The Personal Element in History" as the subject of my "graduating oration" at the University of Rochester, I had been trailing the idea of selfhood. But can the nature of the personal self be learned by any "working over of concepts"? Can we dispense with empirical methods here? Bowne treated as superfluous or worse the endeavours, then beginning, to develop a scientific psychology. But I wanted to know what it had to say, and I assumed that wherever facts can be observed, there the methods of science are imperative. Here is at least a partial explanation of the fact that, though I was for a time absorbed in Bowne's epistemology and metaphysics, the chief effect of my reaction from it was not to induce metaphysical flights of my own, but to develop my interest in the study of man by empirical methods.

Upon becoming responsible for the North-western University department of "philosophy," which as yet included psychology, I promptly introduced a course in what was called "physiological psychology,"

and as soon as possible I brought about the establishment of a laboratory of psychology with an experi-
menter in charge. My own psychological interest
turned for a time to what, in the broadest sense of the
term, has been called the "mystical"—a set of phenomena, involving automatic factors, that reaches all
the way f. om the ouija board and table-tipping to
the experiences of the great Christian and other
religious mystics. To a not inconsiderable extent,
mysticism was becoming a refuge from the disin-
tegrating structure of contemporary theology. Might it
furnish protection from threats that seemed to be
inherent in the scientific movement? Certainly many
persons believed that one could jump over science and
save supernaturalism by having an appropriate
mystical deliverance. This was not the only source
of my interest in mental automatisms, for the study of
them, even at their lower or rudimentary levels,
brought direct enjoyment. But the culmination of
this study is in my published discussions of religious
mysticism. These discussions have a background of
rather minute acquaintance, in considerable measure
experimental, with the conditions, the processes, and
the dynamics of the most common mental automatisms.(18) The foreground, on the other hand, is
analytical inquiry in the field of history and biography.
(16, 19, 4) If one result of these labours was to prove
that there is no real break between mystical and other
experiences, and that mystics have commonly been
mistaken in their off-hand judgments as to the processes

of their own minds, the readers of my works know that I have not failed cordially to recognize the values that have been associated with mystical experiences.

My thinking, as must now be evident, was organizing itself more and more around two foci: the values that life yields, and scientific inquiry into the ways in which the range, the organization, and the security of these values increase and decrease. I am not averse, and I never have been averse, to exercising imagination with respect to possibilities. Rational conduct itself seems to require that we explore, take risks, act at times upon something less than probability. The sciences have no final word as to what is possible. They deal only with what may be expected under "given" conditions, and the "given" in any research is less than the totality of the actual conditions. Room is left, therefore, for the unexpected and the unprecedented. I hardly see, indeed, how anyone can be buoyantly scientific without keeping open what Lowell calls "the soul's east window of divine surprise." But to discriminate between knowledge and imagination, between a partly refractory experience and what we hope for, is necessary to intellectual and ethical health.

Inasmuch as it was my custom to maintain close relations with the ethical and religious interests of students, I had occasion to know how different is the standpoint that I have just described from that which undergraduate students brought to college with them. Their early training at home and in the

Church left most of them unable to make a free and direct judgment upon experienced values, and of course religion and science mixed about as well as oil and water. My endeavours to help undergraduates at such points are represented in a series of addresses and essays entitled *The Religion of a Mature Mind,*(2) in which, of course, I dealt with values, authority, and scientific method. The most delightful—no, *delicious!*—review of this book was one by Campbell Morgan, who condemned it, root and branch. He ended his demurrers by remarking that the title, instead of being *The Religion of a Mature Mind*, might better be *The Irreligion of an Immature Mind.*

The interests that I have described could hardly reach their goal without a comprehensive inquiry into the psychology of religion. I was stimulated thereto, moreover, by two circumstances: the remarkable output of works upon this subject at the turn of the century and soon afterward, and the development of a functional point of view in general psychology. Not only did I need to systematize and round out what I had been doing and what I had been reading, but I felt the need also of a sustained application to religious experience of the new functional mode of investigation. What are people *after* in the various activities that we call religious, and what do these activities really achieve?

A functional analysis of the phenomena called religious depends for its perspective, and therefore for its general truthfulness, so it seemed to me, upon an antecedent, inclusive view of the functions of mind as such. What is mind itself after? What does it want? Current psychology had given only partial and fragmentary answers to this question. The functions commonly attributed to mind are biological; they have to do with the maintenance and the efficiency of the bodily organism, and of man as a biological species. There was far less recognition of mind as having inherent preferences for one or another kind of experience. In an article on "A Proposed Classification of Mental Functions,"(25) I endeavoured to show just what the biological functions of mind are, and then to fill the gap with respect to the preferential functions. The conclusions that I reached in this article are basic to my *Psychology of Religion*.(4) For the main significance of this volume lies in its endeavour to trace out, in religious phenomena, the working of preferences that characterize mind as such. This is the sense in which I treated religion as a natural phenomenon.

Much is involved in saying that mind as such has preferences. It means not only that mental life is selective and purposive in its primary attitudes, but also that it re-works experience, entering thus into the causal grounds of further experience. This implies that mind is not a composite, as scientific psychology in its earlier years represented it to be. Instead, personal selves or potential selves are the very objects that human psychology is all about. Further, from this point of view our native social drives, of which much had been made, seek their terminus in a unity that is based upon and somehow potentially within individually discriminated and approved values, not in herd action and the mechanical and psychical compulsions that it employs.

The particular outcomes of my analysis of the phenomena of religion cannot, of course, be restated here. But something of the trend of the whole may be put into a nutshell. Religion is not something added to the functions that make a man a man, but something already within these functions when they are intensely pursued. To be religious is as natural as it is to be in dead earnest about anything. There are, consequently, as many kinds and levels of religion as there are kinds and levels of society. The key to what is specific in any religious phenomenon is the specific character of the value that is there and then being sought or enjoyed; the key to what is general in religion and the evolution of it is the universally present drive towards being and persisting as a person in a society of persons. Dissatisfaction with achieved values, and revaluation of values—that is, the remaking of ourselves— are among the most characteristic and intense of religious acts. Religious sanctions can attach to anything that men desire, as, for example, the maintenance of a backward and repressive social order. But the prophetic type of religion, in which we see men breaking the shackles imposed by men, reveals a profounder depth in man than appears in any religion that has become conventional. In prophetic religion unprecedented values are conceived, and men set about to make them real. Such religion is not mere subjectivity; it is participation in an objective cosmic process—the creation of man, and of society, and of what used to be called the moral order.

If anyone should care to look for stages in the growth of my thinking towards these conclusions, perhaps the following items, in addition to those already mentioned, might be found significant. The last chapter of *The Spiritual Life*,(1) in which introverted piety is contrasted with an active and extraverted type; an article on "The Sources of the Mystical Revelation,"(16) in which I showed that what seems to be purely individual in the illuminations of mystics is in reality a social product; an article, "Religious Value," (17) in which the view is developed that religion does not contribute to life any new kind of value, but rather operates upon and within values to increase, organize, and perpetuate them; an article on "The Mystical as a Psychological Concept,"(18) in which the higher forms of religious mysticism are put into relation to automatisms in general; finally, an article entitled, "On Having Friends: A Study of Social Values,"(24) which showed that we recognize the existence of ourselves and of other persons primarily by evaluation and action, only secondarily by analysis of phenomena.

The significance of the last point for the psychology of religion is twofold: *First*, religion, as intensification of the functions that most characterize us as persons, participates in the discovery of persons and of society, and thus contributes to an objective and realistic intelligence; *second*, this has a bearing upon faith in divine beings. Religious faith, as distinguished from metaphysical theory, arises not otherwise than through the very same valuational process whereby one recognizes the presence of oneself and of other selves. Men worship because life contains issues that break out of bounds. Every divine figure in the history of religions reflects valuations of human life. The question whether any of these reflections are objectively valid, and if so which ones, never can be answered by theorizing upon facts abstracted from values, but only by entering unreservedly into the valuational process whereby one discovers oneself and one's neighbour. It is an interesting fact that Jesus represented self, neighbour, and God as bound together in experience by one and the same valuational act.

Between this truth and the distress of religion in 1935 there is a relationship that may as well be pointed out now. That faith in God is on the decline is a patent fact. A correlative *and connected* fact is that where the most acute and wide-ranging issues with respect to the value of selfhood and the proper meaning of society are arising, there organized religion, on the whole, is either ambiguous or, at the point of decisive action, hesitant.(36) There is abroad an almost naïve assumption that belief in God depends upon special logical grounds of its own, or else upon a mystical experience that is specifically *ad hoc*.

Meantime, we have war and preparations for war that make the human world look as if there were no God worth considering. Men who believe that they believe in God acquiesce in a nationalism that at the very moment takes the starch out of what belief they have. Comparatively few, even among would-be Christians, have faced the challenge with respect to the value of personality that is presented by our personality-depressing capitalism. Yet it is psychologically preposterous to suppose that without a revolutionary degree of change in our social order the old confident faith can be restored to vigour.(40)

Indeed, why should anyone desire to restore it? The revaluation of selfhood and society that now is upon us, and the breaking up of the old order that is taking place, will mean for our creeds and our theologies either dissolution or else repentance and conversion. What significance the idea of God is to have we cannot even forecast until we have committed ourselves unreservedly to the creation of a new order of society; we shall not know until we experience a new social order in operation. Certain it is that what has been called divine reflects the basic faults and contradictions as well as the virtues of present society. Hence, the widespread anxiety with regard to belief in the divine is a case of misplaced emphasis. What we have now to do is to create, if we can, a mode of human life so meaningful that again our valuations will burst out of bounds.

The identifying of social values, and direct appreciation of them, about which I have now said so much, are so different from accepting the conventionalities of personal goodness in which I was steeped in my childhood and youth that a word is in order with respect to the change in my point of view. Beginning with the early nineties, if not before, my notions of good and evil were shifting towards social relations and the social order. Among the influences that brought about this change, I can identify a few, among them the social-settlement movement, which had recently been inaugurated in England by Arnold Toynbee and in my immediate environment by Jane Addams. Further, in Canon Fremantle, in one of the early works of Shailer Mathews, in Rauschenbusch and in others I caught sight of something in religion that required me to dig deeper. The change in me that I now see to have been inevitable was not abrupt, however. For some years I continued to participate in evangelistic movements among students, hoping each time that the next campaign would "pan out" better than the preceding one. But not one of them fulfilled its promise. At the same period I participated in settlement work for a while; took an active part in local politics (risking my job by opposing some of the intrenched powers); opened social questions with students, and in the new social psychology found a scientific basis for my whole shift in outlook. Social psychology was, in fact, a new thing under the sun, and an important one. Its proof that the individual, *qua* individual, is already part and parcel of society, was an event second in significance to none in the entire history of ethical theory. There is no merely individual good or goodness, no merely individual evil or badness, no merely individual self-determination. The problem of religion, then, from bottom to top, is the problem of the nature, history, outlook, and final significance of persons-realizing-themselves-as-such-in-society.

No wonder that I became absorbed in the problem of education—that is, the formation of personality. A start in this direction was made before the call was issued for the conference out of which the Religious Education Association came to birth. But the movement, of which the association was the chief organized expression and stimulus, provided for my deepest interests an outlet in which I greatly rejoiced. There was much to be investigated, and there was much to be done. There was a psychological problem: How is character formed? There was a theological problem: What, specifically, is the goal of Christianity in respect to the individual-society relation? There was a sociological problem: What is the actual status of personality in our society? Finally, there was a political problem: How is education by the Churches to be co-ordinated with education by the State? The conclusions to which I came cannot be rehearsed here, but the way that the plot deepened upon the stage of my little theatre can be indicated.

In its early stages the religious-education movement aimed at truth in the curriculum (especially truth with respect to the Bible), the selection and gradation of material according to the capacities of pupils, and the use of the best that then was known with respect to method.(3) This was a large undertaking, but it led to a larger one. All the then-existing theories of curriculum and of method assumed that we knew what character is and how it is formed. But neither Church-school leaders nor public-school authorities really knew. The prevalent notion of goodness made it a static combination of elements, qualities, or traits. This notion had to be replaced by insight that character is dynamic, not static; that it is a unit, not a composite, and that it is continuous with the social medium in which it moves.(21) In this whole area we had little more than opinion to go by. Though some opinions were better than others, I felt that teachers should be guided by knowledge, not by rule-of-thumb. Therefore, I took an active part in bringing about some of the outstanding researches in this field.

Soon it appeared that a fresh appraisal must be made of the social significance of our religion. A *fresh* appraisal because it had to be educational for teachers of the young must be concrete, and, if young minds are to assimilate the dynamic essentials, the kernel of each issue must be separated from conventional wrappings. I saw that the teachings of Jesus with respect to love, service, the value of persons, and saving-and-losing life, tend at one and the same point to individualize and to socialize. There is not an individual Gospel plus a social Gospel, but a single Gospel that actually illustrates the nature of personality as social psychology conceives it. The theory of Christian education had to be a social theory, and the practice of Christian education had to be a present exercise of ethical love.(5, 35)

Three things more gradually became clear: *First*, that we have not merely to apply Jesus' teachings, but also to develop germs that were only implicit in them, recognizing problems and developing purposes that were not in his mind at all; *second*, that Christianity will have to reconstruct itself at the same time that it endeavours to bring about reconstruction in society; *third*, that only a creative education can meet the needs here revealed, and that a supposedly Christian education that endeavours first of all to transmit something out of the past will automatically modify its Christian quality towards the vanishing point.(9)

When we inquire into the setting of personality in contemporary society we come upon the disconcerting fact that the overwhelmingly dominant factor is our economic system, and that this system inherently (not merely incidentally) depresses personality in the masses of men, and distorts it in the remainder. This fact is doubly disconcerting; for the discerning teacher of religion must perceive that our Churches as a whole and almost without exception (even of a local sort) ask only for the patching up of this economic system, not for any kind of revolution to end it. Theoretically, the Churches might claim endless life

H

for themselves on the ground of the broadly human principles that they profess. But the truth is that, as yet, the Churches are class institutions standing for the perpetuation of a class economy.(43) This brings their whole future into question, and it leaves to the radically Christian teacher only a narrow ledge upon which to stand and work.

The relation of the Churches to State education has occupied an increasing portion of my attention. Inasmuch as the political power restricts itself to the teaching of so-called secular morality and good citizenship, there falls to the Church *theoretically* the function, not of supplementing State teaching, but of judging it from a more rigorous and more inclusive point of view.(29) If the Church as teacher has any distinctive function with respect to the political order, this function is to stand for radical goodness as against the jostling and compromising of special interests that make up State policy and the background of State teaching. This implies, upon occasion, bold condemnation of the State, to the end that it be ethically rebuilt. I joined my efforts with those of others to induce the Church schools to take a stand like this, and of course I bent my instruction of future ministers, directors of religious education, and Church-school leaders accordingly. But, though a rather amazing change in this direction has begun; though more young people are exposed to social radicalism by the Churches than by all other educational agencies combined, three arresting circumstances confront us:

the Churches reach only a portion of the young, and this a portion selected (unintentionally, of course) on class lines; the Churches, entangled in the ethics of capitalism, are by their inertia if not otherwise resisting radically Christian teaching; and the State schools, and no other school agencies whatsoever, reach practically all the children and most of the younger adolescents of the nation.

For more than ten years now a considerable portion of my puzzlement has concerned the question, What might the State schools do with respect to the depression of personality that our present capitalistic society practices? The young derive their ideas of value and of success, not chiefly from schools, but from the surrounding society—a society that systematically rewards selfishness, demonstrates (as an adolescent of my acquaintance remarked) that "money *is* power," no matter what teachers say; makes possessions the measure of success, and like gamblers and gambling-machines says: "Try your luck." What would be a healthy school in such a sick society?(6) I have reached the conclusion that something—yes, much—can be done by the public schools towards the improvement of life within present society, and even towards the reconstruction of this society. I am convinced, further, that there is an important focal point for any wise endeavour to promote orderly social change and to lessen the horrors of the disorderly change that appears to be approaching. (10, 44).

Does my present and recent preoccupation with social problems, largely economic and political, indicate that a mind that once was absorbed in religious interests has degenerated into secularism? My own interpretation of what has happened is that I have grown realistic with respect to the spiritual concerns that interested me at the beginning. The spiritual is present wherever persons are present; and whatever, from milk to roses, and from a game of tag to a pay envelope, gives colour or form to a personali+y, is a concern of any religion that would be realistica ly spiritual. To be utterly devoted to whatever in heaven or earth is personal is to be religiously consecrate. Between my earlier printed contributions to religious education and the psychology of religion, on the one hand, and on the other hand my later articles, most of which have to do with the social question directly, I see, if not growth, at least forward movement towards an old goal. Nor do I think that the goal of religion or of theology can be reached otherwise than by deeper and still deeper immersion into the concrete actualities of economic society with a view to a revolutionary change.

Current efforts to save Christian faith by turning away from the economic tragedy to something else are of many sorts. They include private mystical practices and "enriched" worship (as early as 1923 I was sure that the movement for the enrichment of worship is self-deceived);(30, 39) re-emphasis upon the depravity of the human heart, and upon our alleged helplessness and dependence upon God; reversion from the idea of a world-mastering faith to adoration of an Absolute, holy and self-contained, who does not come down into the dust of industrialism; finally, reliance upon the practice of Christ-like self-giving in face-to-face relations to do all that needs to be done. These endeavours either to get above the economic issue or to reach it by an oblique goodness do not avail. Capitalism has no serious objection to such religion. The religious and the theological emergency can be met only by thought-structures and practices to which capitalism does object because they threaten its existence.

In the economic sphere, then, the great drama of the soul is being played to-day. Opportunity for private profit is opportunity for one person, by virtue of the sole fact of superior material possessions, to control other persons; and the result is division of society into classes, multiplied injustices, and ever stiffer organization of the modern national, war-making states. If we are to give effect to the Christian belief in the value of persons, then, we must commit ourselves to the active struggle for a classless society, including the economic conditions without which such a society cannot come into being.

At the present moment I am wrestling with a growing realization that our inherited ethical principles, though they contain a premonition of this goal, are incapable of guiding us to it. It is true that a profoundly radical germ always has been harboured

within Christianity; yet Christian ethics, like secular
ethics, never has concerned itself with how to carry on
a social revolution. Plenty of religionists are eager
to tell us what not to do, but it is steam, not brakes,
that moves a train up a gradient. As a matter of fact,
to what extent are current cautions against revolutionary haste derived from anti-revolutionary assumptions unconsciously held? In any case, our virtue
will reside in what we do and dare, not in what we
refrain from doing. We need to warn ourselves,
moreover, that any valid "Thou shalt not" must not
only have the same ultimate ground as some "Thou
shalt"; it must be secondary thereto and derived from
it. Good sentiments on the positive side united with
conduct-inhibitions on the negative side never made
a good man nor a tenable religious ethics.(45)

Where, then, can we look for light on how to carry
on a revolution? I think there is at least a glimmer in
the New Testament. Is it, for instance, a duty to see
that hunger, when it assumes mass proportions, is
fed and then prevented from recurring? If so, can
the Christian duty of feeding the hungry be fulfilled
until the masses of men have established a right
to take the food that they need? Is not an ethics of
mere giving-and-receiving illusory because ineffective,
and is it, in fact, consonant with the respect for
personality that we profess? This will illustrate a
surmise of mine that we need to develop realistically
several of the revolutionary implications of New
Testament principles that already are upon our lips.(41)

But I do not think that we middle-class intellectuals have in ourselves or in history sufficient resources to solve the problem of our own duty. We must seek light upon it in addition by going straight to the discontented masses, endeavouring to see through their eyes. According to our traditions, we should be the teachers of the masses, telling them what their proper place is, and how to conduct themselves when they are grievously injured. But tradition shatters upon fact. We are not their teachers, nor shall we be. It is time for us to humble ourselves and take the attitude of learners. Light, not merely heat, is radiating from the refusal of workers to accept their lot. They will make mistakes, as all men do (even intellectuals!), and the methods of revolution that they employ will require scrutiny; but the awakening of the workers is *per se* an ethical awakening; their insistence is an ethical imperative, and, on the main point, they will not go wrong.

To the proletariat, then, I am looking for light—for light upon the religious life! This means, among other things, that my faith, which has survived many vicissitudes by consenting to be modified—and, as I think, enriched—by them, is again acquiring an unaccustomed perspective. I can best indicate what this perspective is by twisting a passage of Scripture out of its primary meaning:

> God chose the foolish things of the world,
> that he might put to shame them that are wise;
> and God chose the weak things of the world,

that he might put to shame the things that are strong:
and the base things of the world,
and the things that are despised,
did God choose,
yea and the things that are not,
that he might bring to nought the things that are.

My career is now so near its close that the only great new experience that I have a right to expect is that of dying. I hope, and for many years have hoped, that this event will take place in full consciousness and with a clear understanding of what is happening. My desire to watch the flickering out of the candle originated, perhaps, in mere curiosity, but it has become an aspect of a new outlook—new to me and to those who have commented upon my essay, "A Realistic View of Death."(38)

Most persons, it appears, whenever they contemplate the fact that they are moving towards their own death, become introverted (if they were not so already). They shudder over the idea; are unwilling to think about it; adopt devices for shunting their attention, perhaps smother the plain fact in imaginative compensation-hopes for a future life, or in speculations about it. As against all this, a cool implacable objectivity of mind seems to be desirable. Perhaps dying has, or might acquire, values that we miss when we practise this shrinking introversion. I am not in the attitude of throwing old faiths and hopes to the wind, even though they contain this element of introversion, but I am convinced that the problem of death should be approached from a different angle. What our traditional approaches lack is an ethical realism that corresponds to the realism of the physician and of the psychologist. This means that we must discern values where they occur, and that we must open a way for experimental endeavours to increase values.

Death certainly has values—values so great that if we could not die we should be doomed to a less satisfactory existence than the present one. These values, I hold, we might increase by deliberate planning, and an individual, by voluntary participation in such planning, might actually incorporate dying into his life-purposes. What is called "dissolution" or "the end," and is treated as if it were a physical event like the stopping of an electric current by an automatic switch, would then become an ethical event wherein the flow of ethical energy in the world is actually increased.

My essay is a preliminary and tentative exploration of this uncharted territory. Unreservedly recognizing that the frailty of human life presents what appears to be a set of ethical surds, I have shown that this is only a part of the truth; that both society and the individual gain by our mortality; that we can increase these gains, and that some individuals whom I have observed achieved a mastery of their own death without waiting for the experience of a future life—even without expecting it. My acquaintance with such instances has increased since the essay was printed. If, now, this be the case with what Christian tradition conceives as "the last great enemy," then the natural order, which has us in its inexorable grasp, is more like an ethical order than theology and philosophy have realized.

BIBLIOGRAPHY

BOOKS

(1) *The Spiritual Life: Studies in the Science of Religion.* New York. 1900.
 The same in Danish translation. Copenhagen. 1907.

(2) *The Religion of a Mature Mind.* Chicago. 1902.

(3) *Education in Religion and Morals.* Chicago. 1904.
 The same in Spanish translation. Buenos Aires. 1919.
 The same in Chinese translation. Shanghai. 1920.

(4) *The Psychology of Religion.* Chicago. 1916.
 The same in Japanese translation. Tokio. 1925.

(5) *A Social Theory of Religious Education.* New York. 1917.
 The same in Japanese translation. 1932.

(6) *Law and Freedom in the School: "Can and Cannot," "Must and Must Not," "Ought and Ought Not," in Pupil's Projects.* Chicago. 1924. Pp. ix+133.

(7) *What Ails Our Youth?* New York. 1924.

(8) *The Motives of Men.* New York. 1928.

(9) *What Is Christian Education?* New York. 1929.

(10) *Educating for Citizenship.* New York. 1932.

ARTICLES IN PERIODICALS AND CHAPTERS IN BOOKS OF COMPOSITE AUTHORSHIP

NOTE.—I have included here only such articles and chapters as seem most likely to reveal the trend of my thought at different periods. *Religious Education*, vol. xxii, pp. 443–7, publishes a much more extended list of productions up to 1926.

(11) A study in the dynamics of personal religion. *Psychological Review*, 1899, pp. 484–505.

(12) Methods of studying religion. *Methodist Review*, 1901, pp. 532–47.

(13) Religion as a factor in individual and social development. *Biblical World*, 1904, pp. 37–47.

(14) The philosophy of the movement for religious education. *American Journal of Theology*, 1904, pp. 225–39.

(15) Articles in Hastings' *Encyclopaedia of Religion and Ethics* as follows:
Adolescence, vol. i, pp. 101–3.
Childhood, vol. iii, pp. 518–21.
Growth, moral and religious, vol. vi, pp. 445–50.
Infancy, vol. vii, pp. 278–9.
Morbidness, vol. viii, pp. 841–2.

(16) The sources of the mystical revelation. *Hibbert Journal*, 1908, pp. 359–72.

(17) Religious value. *Journal of Philosophy*, 1908, pp. 253–6.

(18) The mystical as a psychological concept. *Journal of Philosophy*, 1909, pp. 197–202.

(19) Religion and the subconscious. *American Journal of Theology*, 1909, pp. 337–49.

(20) The idea of God. *Religious Education*, 1911, pp. 175–84.

(21) Virtue and the virtues; a study of method in the teaching of morals. *Proceedings of the National Education Association*, 1911, pp. 419–25; *Religious Education*, 1912, pp. 485–92.

(22) Religious education. Monroe's *Cyclopaedia of Education*, vol. v, pp. 145–50.

(23) Sunday schools in the United States, education status of. Monroe's *Cyclopaedia of Education*, vol. v, pp. 452–62.

(24) On having friends: a study of social values. *Journal of Philosophy*, 1915, pp. 155–61.

(25) A proposed classification of mental functions. *Psychological Review*, 1915, pp. 87–98.

(26) Contemporary ideals in religion. Chapter x of *Ideals of America*, Chicago, 1919, pp. 239–59; also in *Religious Education*, 1916, pp. 377–87.

(27) The religious breakdown of the ministry. *Journal of Religion*, 1921, pp. 18–29.

(28) Opposing theories of the curriculum. *Religious Education*, 1922, pp. 143–50.

(29) Religious education and political conscience. *Teachers' College Record*, 1922, pp. 297–304; also in *Religious Education*, 1922, pp. 430–5.

(30) Who is enriched by the enrichment of worship? *Journal of Religion*, 1923, pp. 22–33.

(31) Youth and Peace. *Scribner's Magazine*, 1925, pp. 8–13; printed also in *Essays of 1925*, Odell Shepard, editor. Hartford, 1926, pp. 65–76.

(32) Problematic factors in the concept of moral education. *School and Society*, 1926, pp. 505–9.

(33) Psychology and the scientific study of religion; and, Christian faith in the light of psychology. Chapters viii and ix of *An Outline of Christianity*, vol. iv, pp. 95–128.

(34) Academic liberty in denominational colleges. *School and Society*, 1929, pp. 678–80.

(35) What makes a college Christian? *Christian Education*, 1930, pp. 8–15.

(36) What's coming in religion? The main stream and the eddies. *Christian Century*, 1930, pp. 1619–22.

(37) The War Department as educator. Published, 1930, by the Committee on Militarism in Education.

(38) A realistic view of death. Chapter vii in *Religious Realism*, D. C. Macintosh, editor. New York, 1931.

(39) The social value of prayer and worship. *World To-morrow*, 1932, pp. 175–7.

(40) Why religion is anxious. *World To-morrow*, 1932, pp. 326–7.

(41) What is violence? *World To-morrow*, 1932, pp. 378–9.

(42) Two kinds of coercion. *World To-morrow*, 1933, pp. 177–9.

(43) What capitalism does to Protestantism. *World To-morrow*, 1933, pp. 374–5.

(44) Education as social engineering. *The Social Frontier*, 1935, pp. 25–9.

(45) When pacifism turns sectarian. *Christian Century*, 1935, pp. 429–30.

From Credence to Faith

by

ALFRED LOISY

Honorary Professor in the Collège de France

Translated by M. D. P.

PREFACE

HE who writes the following lines was brought up
a Roman Catholic, and received, in his early years, a
religious education quite immune from the influence
of that rationalism which has, ever since the eighteenh
century, been continually at war with Catholicism
as established in France. Of that rationalism, often
sectarian in character, the author may say that he has
never been a disciple. He has nevertheless reached,
through the various experiences of his existence, a
religious faith which attributes, indeed, to Christianity a place of eminence amongst the religions of
the world, but which also recognizes in all ancient
religions, even the most primitive, some part in the
education of mankind; for to the mind of this author
all these religions seem destined finally to be fused in
a higher religion, adapted to the needs of a spiritually
unified humanity.

I. RELIGIOUS VOCATION [1]

I was born February 28, 1857, in a village of Cham-
pagne (Ambrières, Marne, district Vitry-le-François),

[1] For the documentation of this part see my *Mémoires pour
servir à l'histoire religieuse de notre temps* (1931), vol. I, pp. 9–91.

of a traditionally Catholic family, whose members had, from father to son, been agricultural workers[1] in that same region. Their mentality, towards the middle of the last century, was still, in many respects, that of the peasants of the *ancien régime*, before 1789. I should have followed the same profession if a serious illness, before I was two years old, had not rendered me permanently unfit for labour in the fields. As I soon manifested a natural facility for study my parents decided, when I was twelve years old, to place me in a secondary school. They did not contemplate an ecclesiastical profession, nor did I think of it myself, though I piously fulfilled the religious duties which were customary at my age in the good Catholic families of our midst. I began therefore my classical studies in April 1869, in the municipal college of Vitry-le-François. I did not much care for the lay spirit that reigned in the house, and the life of a boarder was particularly disagreeable to me. The war of 1870–1 restored me to my family; in 1871–2 I continued my studies under the tuition of the *curé* of my village, and I then went to the Ecclesiastical College of St.-Dizier, where I stayed two years, 1872–4. The first notion of a sacerdotal vocation came to me the very day on which the *curé*, whom I have mentioned, was installed in the church of Ambrières; when I saw him mount the altar I had a lively impression that I myself would, one day,

[1] The French expression is *cultivateurs*—implying rather peasant possession than paid labour.

mount that same altar to say Mass. But this was only a presentiment, not a resolution. My decision was made in October 1873, during a retreat preached in the Chapel of the College of St.-Dizier by Father Stumpf, former rector of the College of St. Clement at Metz. I was struck by what this Jesuit said to us about "election,"[1] about the choice to be made between God and the world. Having no taste for any secular profession, I determined to give myself to God, and as soon as the scholastic year was completed I began, in spite of the objections of my family, to put my design into action by arranging to enter the seminary of Châlons-sur-Marne.

I received the ecclesiastical habit at the beginning of October 1874, and from the first the regular life of the seminary charmed me; I gave myself up with ardour to the exercises of piety that we had to practise, above all to the morning's meditation. Nevertheless I was troubled by certain things which I failed to understand. The Vatican Council had just taken place, and everybody knew that the Bishop of Châlons, Mgr. Meignan, was amongst those who regarded the definition of papal infallibility as inopportune. In the professorial body of the seminary, and among my co-disciples, there were ultramontanes and liberals. Without measuring the exact importance of these dissensions I had imagined the Church more wholly one in her spirit, and if I found myself amongst the

---

[1] Term used in the *Exercises of St. Ignatius* for the choice of a vocation.

liberals it was because I had confidence in my professor of philosophy, whom I had chosen as my confessor, and who was regarded as a liberal.

Now my room neighbour was a young man whose health had prevented him from becoming a monk in the Order of Preachers, and who intended to join the Third Order of Teachers of St. Dominic. It seemed to me that my place should rather be in such an institution than in parochial ministry. My admission to the novitiate was already arranged in principle when my confessor, with the support of my family, persuaded me to a delay which I regarded as provisional, but which further circumstances rendered definitive.

Grave difficulties arose in my mind during the course of the following year—1875–6—when I came into contact with the dogmatic and moral doctrines of the Church. This theology was not the abstruse scholasticism which was soon to prevail in the teaching of all the French seminaries. Its metaphysics still had a tincture of Cartesianism, like the philosophy of M. Manier (Renan's master at St.-Sulpice), which had been taught me in the preceding year. But if M. Manier's philosophy had cast no trouble in my mind it was not so with the theology of M. Bouvier, who died Bishop of Mans. It was not that logic was lacking from his system; everything was proved by Scripture, the Fathers of the Church, and reason; but it was a reason that worked upon accepted tradition. The foundation of the structure was a divine testimony, which seemed to carry its own recommendation as an indisputable revelation. The means for radical criticism were not at my disposal, but I soon experienced an abiding sense, almost an obsession, of non-objectivity, in face of a demonstration whose force was not greater than that which Bossuet's *Discours sur l'histoire universelle* would have for us to-day.

This sense of insecurity was only increased when I came to study the theological *Summa* of St. Thomas Aquinas and his *Summa contra Gentiles*, their display of superficial logic being more considerable, while the basis was no more solid. I endeavoured to believe that these involuntary doubts were diabolical temptations or scruples, and that they would disappear of themselves as my director, to whom I confided them, thought. I had, besides, devised a distraction which was, eventually, to be a potent factor in the solution of my perplexities, and that was the study of Hebrew, which I undertook without a master, and simply in order to read the books of the Old Testament in their original tongue. I confined myself to a comparison of the Massoretic text, the version of the Septuaginta (in the Sixtine edition) and the Vulgate (in the Clementine edition). Provisionally this work could not be other than a rest to my mind; I had no least suspicion that it was shaping my future.

It is not hard to understand that, under these conditions, and according to the advice of my director, I was able in conscience, though not without some

interior anguish, to receive the clerical tonsure and
minor orders June 25, 1877, then the subdiaconate,
June 30, 1878; I did not feel that I had the right nor,
still less, the duty to turn back. Thus it came about
that I was sent to Paris, in October 1878, to follow
the course of the Faculty of Theology which had just
been instituted in the Catholic University. I was
there for three months, and this first contact with the
higher teaching of theology plunged me into such a
state of fatigue that, when I returned to my family
for the New Year holidays, the doctor, who had
attended me from childhood, forbade me to go back
to Paris for a time. I returned, therefore, after some
weeks of complete rest to the Seminary of Châlons,
where I was ordained deacon on March 29, 1879, and
priest (with a dispensation for being under the
canonical age) on June 29, 1879. I entered on the
parochial ministry as village *curé* at the end of July,
and remained until May 1881, just long enough to
assure myself that I was not suited to this ministry,
and that, now that my health was sufficiently restored,
I ought to return to Paris to take my theological
degrees and prepare for a career of teaching. I took
this course with some hesitation, but I did not see how
else I could follow a useful and congenial career.
And I may also note that, while pursuing in solitude
the meditations and labours I had commenced in the
Great Seminary, I had conceived the plan of writing
a general apology of Roman Catholicism; an apology
which, at that time, could be nothing other than a

defence of Catholicism against my own anxieties and scruples, which had not been laid to rest.

11. THE BREAKDOWN OF ORTHODOXY[1]

In devoting myself to scientific religious studies I was undertaking the exploration of an unknown land which was to bring me many a surprise. It was, above all, thanks to Abbé Louis Duchesne (later Mgr. Duchesne) that I was kept at the Catholic Institute of Paris, to teach Hebrew in the first place. At the end of 1881, when the professor of Holy Scripture and Hebrew fell ill, Duchesne proposed me to the rector, Mgr. d'Hulst, as repetitor of Hebrew to my co-disciples. This was the modest beginning of a career of teaching which, with progressive developments, lasted for twelve years. But my orthodoxy began to fail during the course of this period, and it will be well to mark, here, the successive stages.

Duchesne had lent me, in July 1881, the volume of the Gospels in the great Tischendorf edition, to study during the holidays, so that I might learn therefrom the scientific method of editing ancient texts. Instead of confining myself to the construction of the critical apparatus I ventured on to a comparison of the varying recensions of the Gospels on the same point; amongst others of the narratives of the resurrection of Christ. There it seemed to me that the diver-

[1] For this part of the notice the principal documentation is in the *Mémoires*, vol. i, pp. 92–154.

gences touched the very basis of the documents, but I did not draw the final consequences of my observation. I concluded that if Divine inspiration guaranteed the truth of the Scriptures it did not guarantee the exactitude of their information, even on very important points.

Other experiences completed this one. During the scholastic year, 1881–2, I followed at St.-Sulpice, as student, the course of M. Vigouroux, in which he defended the Holy Scripture against rationalistic criticism. He there proved, with learning, that Noah's Ark, according to its dimensions, could easily lodge couples of every animal species living on the earth. This apologetic showed me, above all, that the traditional conception of Biblical truth could not be defended, and that the claims of Protestant and rationalistic criticism were, in part, justified.

At the commencement of the scholastic year of 1882–3, it being decided that I should remain at the Catholic Institute and prepare to teach the Sacred Scripture later on, I put down my name for the courses of Assyriology and Egyptology that were given at the École pratique des Hautes Études, and, by the advice of superiors and confessor, I followed also the course in Hebrew that Renan was giving at the Collège de France. Renan was commenting on the Psalms, especially from the point of view of textual criticism, though all the rest followed naturally. It was not the general opinions of Renan that first influenced me—his *Histoire du peuple d'Israël* only appeared later—but I became thoroughly impregnated with his method, even though I flattered myself that I could refute him with his own weapons—which I never did, at least in the sense I had in mind; for Renan, as a critic of the Bible, was always rather too circumspect than the contrary. Renan taught me to examine the texts of the Bible scientifically, and what I inferred from his lessons was that the scientific commentary of the Bible, in the Catholic Church, had to be recast from its foundation if it was to be adapted to the actual condition of contemporary culture.

I did not at first perceive that this conclusion was the ruin of the whole economy of the theological tradition of the Roman Church, and that it fundamentally compromised certain dogmas; I even contemplated a general reform of Catholic teaching, founded on a notion of the relativity of these beliefs, which would preserve the substance of these superannuated doctrines. Thus I elaborated, during the scholastic year of 1883–4, two theses of modest volume which I hoped to present for the doctorate of theology in our Faculty: one on the idea of Biblical inspiration suggested by the sacred writers themselves and the more ancient of the Fathers;[1] the other, directly inspired by Renan's lectures, on the textual criticism of the Psalms.[2] The first of these two theses was the

[1] "De divina Scripturarum inspiratione quid doceant ipsae Scripturae" (*inédit*).

[2] "La version grecque des Psaumes, dite version des Septante, et le texte massorétique" (*inédit*).

most important. In the first part it was shown that the
exegesis practised by the writers of the New Testament on the texts of the Old was purely arbitrary
and to be explained by the impossibility of interpreting
history according to the original sense of the texts;
in the second part it was shown that the exegesis of
the ancient Fathers was no less arbitrary, whence
followed a notion of relative truth both for these
exegetical books and for the contents of the Bible
itself, with, at the same time, a justification of the
living *magisterium* of the Church, as conceived by
the antagonists of Gnosticism, Irenaeus, and Tertul-
lian; such a *magisterium* as the very imperfections
of Scripture and tradition rendered indispensable. The
only man to whom I communicated my manuscript,
Mgr. d'Hulst, begged me to bury it in the safest
drawer of my writing-table (where it yet is), as it
would be ill understood by theologians. It was
impossible for me not soon to realize the radical
incompatibility of my general conclusions from
critical experience with Roman orthodoxy. An incident which occurred during my course of exegesis
in March 1885 began to enlighten me on this point.
While commenting the first chapters of Isaiah I came
to the famous prophecy of Emmanuel (Isa. vii. 14)
and explained that this passage, in itself, was not an
announcement of the virginal conception of Christ,
but of the coming birth of a child, perhaps Ezechias,
and that the interpretation given of it in the First
Gospel (Matt. i. 22–23) was a kind of spiritual and

providential accommodation. At the following lesson one of my auditors, from St.-Sulpice, brought me a cleverly constructed questionary, but entirely theological in character; as though the author—certainly one of the directors of the Seminary of St.-Sulpice —knowing that I had disputed the direct applicability of the prophetical text to the birth of Jesus—ignored, or wished to ignore, the reasons by which I had established the true sense of the text, and the kind of justification I had proposed of the Gospel interpretation. I was soon made aware that the Superior General of St.-Sulpice judged my conclusions to be theologically reprehensible.

But it was, above all, by the work of my own mind that I realized the failure of traditional orthodoxy and the extreme difficulty, or moral impossibility, of mending it. This became evident to me in December 1885 and January 1886, but without my coming to deny—an important point to note just here—the substantial and fundamental truth of the Christian and Catholic tradition. Here are the terms in which I summed up my religious position in a note of November 15, 1886.[1]

"I am determined to work for the service of that Church which has been and is responsible for the education of humanity. Without denying her tradition, but on the condition of retaining its spirit rather than its letter, she remains, for me, a necessary institution, and the most divine on earth. She has capitalized

[1] *Mémoires,* vol. i, p. 151.

the subtleties of theologians, but she has also amassed those principles of order, devotion, and virtue which guarantee family happiness and social peace. To seek to found anything in the moral order outside Christ and the Church would be, in these days, a pure Utopia. That there are superannuated elements of ecclesiastical discipline, practices of worship not in harmony with the needs of the day, that the material sense of theological formulas is becoming daily less defensible, all this is becoming more and more clear to me as I get better acquainted with the past of religion and of humanity. I may be deceived, and I remain, as regards my will, fully disposed to admit the contrary of what I now think if the contrary of what I think be true."

Certainly I should not now write, without many reservations, that the Church has been the educatress of humanity. But I am here setting forth my dispositions in 1886. I thought it not only my duty, but still more my right, to remain in the Church, and serve her, according to my means, in the compromising situation in which I saw her. I *could* remain in the Church because I believed in her unique providential mission to mankind and in the substantial worth of her doctrine. I thought I *ought* to remain in the Church because I believed myself to be bound to her by the engagements of the priesthood, and I did not think I had the right to break the promise I had made to consecrate my life to her. I had given that life for the service of humanity, as upheld by the Church, and

I did not think I had any right to take back my gift, so long as the Church herself was disposed to employ me usefully and honourably. I ventured to hope that she would not obstinately refuse to participate, prudently and wisely, in the work of all the seekers after truth who exist in the world, and amongst whom I hoped to take my place. Thus I could remain in the Church in good faith, without abusing the confidence that the ecclesiastical authorities and my Catholic friends might have in me. I thus explain the various initiatives on which I ventured in the movement termed Modernist, and also my attitude in regard to the censures that followed on my writings. I endured those disciplinary censures while reserving my scientific liberty, and I did not quit the Roman Church until she herself solemnly declared that I no longer belonged to her.

III. THE MODERNIST PHASE[1]

I was in no haste to give effect to my projects for a Catholic reform; I applied myself for a long time to positive research, while waiting for an occasion to enter on important problems. In the spring of 1889 I was in a position to accept or refuse the Chair of Sacred Scripture, which was offered me for the

[1] For this part see *Mémoires*, vol. i, pp. 155–557, and all vol. ii. My principal publications of that period will be signalled in the course of the present narrative. It will be impossible to mention in detail the bibliographical articles I gave to the *Bulletin critique* from 1882 to 1900, and to the *Revue critique d'histoire et de littérature* from 1889 to 1927.

scholastic year of 1889–90. Duchesne was averse
to my accepting it. He was already possessed by the
idea, to which he adhered until his death, of the utter
impossibility of any scientific evolution of Biblical
learning in the Roman Church; he foresaw the permanent, and already imminent, danger to which I
should expose myself in undertaking responsibility
for a teaching that would bring me into conflict
with theologians; on the other hand he pointed out
the advantages and facilities of an honourable career
in the domain of Semitic philology, with its promise
of the paradise of the learned, a chair in the Institut
de France. And, in fact, I could, by abstaining from
the treatment of religious questions, have acquired
a high position as a Catholic savant. But this kind of
glory was never a temptation to me, and I chose my
part, which was to undertake, prudently and methodi-
cally, the reform of Biblical teaching in the Roman
Church, or, at bottom, the moral reform of the intellectual system of Roman Catholicism.

My plan of teaching was simple and clear, and vast
enough to occupy my whole life had I been left free
to fulfil it. My fundamental idea was to create a scientific study of the Bible in the Catholic Church by
transposing questions of Biblical introduction and
exegesis from the dogmatic and artificial scheme of
scholastic theology into the definite scheme of criticism and history. Hence my programme demanded,
for each scholastic year, a general question of introduction, and the exegesis of a Biblical book, or con-

siderable part of one; the whole eventually constituting a history and critical commentary of the Bible.

My point of departure was the actual state of ecclesiastical beliefs: the Bible is the collection of books which the Church regards and has regarded as divinely inspired. Hence the first question to be treated would be, logically, the origin, perpetuity, and actual definition of the nature of divine inspiration, and how this conception was to be regarded from the point of view of historical and philosophical criticism.[1]

The second question was as follows: Given that certain books are said to be inspired, and thus constitute a divinely authorized collection, called the Canon of the Scriptures, under what conditions, whether as regards the Jewish Scriptures, called the Old Testament, or as regards the Christian Scriptures, called the New Testament, was this collection made and preserved, and what is the ancient and historical authority for these collections, termed canonical and regarded as normative?

The third question was as to the languages in which these books had been composed or into which they had been translated, as to the means and conditions by which they had been preserved and transmitted to us, and as to the measure in which the transmitted text could be guaranteed.

The fourth question was this: when, how, by whom

[1] This is developed in the programme of the review *L'Enseignement biblique*, 1892. I had founded this review as an organ of my own teaching; it only survived two years, 1892–3.

and to what end were these books drawn up; or, rather, what character and what authenticity can we attribute to them?

The fifth question was: What teaching can we draw from these books as to the ancient history of Israel and the birth of Christianity, as to the history of the religious ideas of the Jews and those of the first Christians, as to that of the religious institutions of Judaism and those of ancient Christianity?

The sixth question (which I could as well have placed after the third) was: What has been drawn from these books; according to what principles did the Jews interpret the Hebraic Bible; how has the Christian Church interpreted, and how does she still interpret the documents of her faith, in the two Testaments; how, in these latter days, has a critical and historical exegesis detached itself from the traditional and theological exegesis, and has it acquired autonomy in its methods and conclusions?

All this would not imply six distinct histories, but six parts or aspects of one same history, no part being independent of the other, and all being explanatory one of another. All these questions entered into the separate study of each of the Biblical books. It was inopportune to touch first on the question of Biblical inspiration, and I therefore kept it back. During the four years that I taught the Sacred Scriptures I studied the history of the Biblical Canon, and that of the version and texts of the Old Testament;[1] I commented Proverbs;[2] the Book of Job;[3] the first chapters of Genesis;[4] the first chapters of the Synoptic Gospels.[5] The barrier of orthodoxy seemed to me the less formidable because orthodoxy has changed ceaselessly even while declaring itself unchangeable. And, as regarded the objections to be drawn from the dogma of inspiration, I said to myself: The Sacred Books are inspired unto truth, but they are what they are, let us know what they are in order to know the truth which they contain. As to the difficulties raised in the name of tradition, I continued to distinguish between the historical sense and ecclesiastical interpretation.[6]

There is no need to retrace in detail the events which prevented me from realizing my programme. In October 1892 the Superior of St.-Sulpice, M. Icard, forbade his students to attend my course of Sacred Scripture because I had contested the historical character of the first books of Genesis. After that the Rector of the Institut Catholique, Mgr. d'Hulst, flattering himself that he would enlighten ecclesiastical

[1] *Histoire du Canon de l'Ancien Testament* (1890). *Histoire du Canon du Nouveau Testament* (1891). *Histoire critique du texte et des versions de l'Ancien Testament*, except the Vulgate, in *Enseignement biblique*, 1892–3.

[2] The Introduction only was published in the *Revue des Religions*, 1890.

[3] *Enseignement biblique*, 1892.

[4] Unpublished.

[5] *Enseignement Biblique*, 1893.

[6] See "La Critique biblique" (opening lecture for 1892–3) in *Enseignement biblique*, 1892; reproduced in the collection *Les Études bibliques*, 1894–1901–1903.

opinion on the subject, treated of the "Question biblique" in the *Correspondant* of January 25, 1893, and
approached it on its least actual and most dangerous
side, that of inspiration. A violent and confused
controversy arose, in which I took no part, but which
resulted in the Council of the Episcopal Protectors of
the Institute withdrawing me from the teaching of
the Sacred Scripture, and eventually, when I had
myself explained the true Biblical question in a very
moderate article, "La Question biblique et l'inspiration des Écritures,"[1] from the teaching also of Hebrew
and Assyrian (November 1893).

The principal consequence of all this was that, being
now relegated to a chaplaincy in a convent school of
young girls at Neuilly-sur-Seine, I took, as theme of
my thoughts and preoccupations, the ordinary
teaching of the Church, and not only the history of
the Bible. Ever since the Encyclical *Providentissimus
Deus* of Leo XIII on Biblical studies, in November
1893, pontifical acts had been multiplied which
strengthened the intransigent position of official
theology. There was a new constitution of the Index
(*Officiorum et Munerum*, January 25, 1897); a Decree
of the Holy Office (January 15, 1897) declaring the
authenticity of the verse of the Three Celestial Wit-
nesses in the first Epistle of St. John; an Encyclical of
Leo XIII to the Clergy of France (September 1899),
in which exegetical innovators were reprehended.

---

[1] *Enseignement biblique*, 1893, and reproduced in the three
editions of *Études bibliques*.

But all these manifestations, far from discouraging me, excited me to fresh activity. The Bibliographical reviews with which I collaborated (the *Bulletin critique*, and above all the *Revue critique*) furnished me with all the books useful to my research. Besides which, in order to keep up direct contact with the public, with the help of friends, I founded in 1896 the *Revue d'histoire et de littérature religieuses*, which survived until 1907, and the object of which was purely historical and critical. Besides which I was interested in certain writings of Newman, in particular the *Essay on the Development of Christian Doctrine*, and in some Protestant works which made a sensation at the time—the *Lehrbuch der Dogmen Geschichte* of Harnack (1885–97) and the *Esquisse d'une philosophie de la Religion* of Auguste Sabatier (1897). It was thus that in 1897–9 I elaborated a new programme of Catholic renovation in opposition to Roman intransigence, which I first entitled *Essais d'histoire et de critique religieuses*, and, in a second redaction, *Essais d'histoire et de philosophie religieuses*.

Here is an extract of the plan (*Mémoires*, vol. i, pp. 444–6):

A religious science is in process of formation outside and against Catholicism. A religious science should be instituted also within the Church and for her. . . . This work is not one of learned history, nor profound philosophy, nor transcendental theology, nor triumphant apologetic; it is . . . above all a sincere expression of the contemporary religious problem in so far as the author has been able to apprehend it. He has endeavoured, as far as he could, to interpret the testimony that historical science renders to religion and to determine the character and extent of that testimony; to seek the foundation of certainty in religious and moral belief, the economy of faith and the mission of the Church; and, lastly, to show, not only the permanent solution that Catholicism offers of the religious problem, but also the duty of Catholicism to realize this mission more fully and efficaciously by the adoption of a programme of action which would be immediate and not a vague future promise.

The book thus announced comprised twelve chapters in two parts; the seven chapters of the first part dealt respectively with the general theories of religion and Christianity (beginning with the official thesis of Catholic demonstration as defined by the Vatican Council); there was a special discussion of the ideas of religion and revelation, the history of Jewish monotheism, the Gospel of Jesus, the organic evolution of the Church, her doctrinal evolution, her ritual evolution. The four first chapters of the second part treated of the intellectual *régime* of Roman Catholicism, of dogma and science, reason and faith, religion and life.

"On all these points," I wrote (*Mémoires*, vol. i, pp. 447), "a certain progress seems possible, desirable, and inevitable sooner or later; the final chapter (twelfth) will be an expression of confidence and hope in the future of Catholicism."

It may be observed that the general point of view of this synthesis is chiefly historical, and that the problem, for example, of God, as presented by the progress of natural science, is hardly indicated. But, whatever its deficiencies, the work had not time to come to light. Some fragments only appeared in a Catholic review—"Le développement chrétien d'après le Cardinal Newman" (*Revue du Clergé français,* December 1, 1898), in which I noted that the principle of development applied by Newman "to the history of Christianity in its relation to the Gospel is applicable to the Gospel in its relation to Judaism, and to the Mosaic religion in its relation to all that preceded it"; that is to say, "to the entire history of religion since the beginning of mankind."

In the same review (January 1, 1899) on *"La Théorie individualiste de la religion* of A. Sabatier" I spoke of "the partial definition of the Christian religious sentiment" in its belief in God the Father, who forgives sin, but that "to speak of religion is to speak of something other than individualism; religion, in its most imperfect forms, having always sought the union of *mankind*, and not just the union of *man* with God."

In the same review (June 1, 1899), in an article called "La Définition de la religion," it is maintained that "reason and history teach us that the social character is essential to any definition of religion"; and that "religion is not a childish explanation of the world," since the religions that exist or have existed "have always had a cult before having a cosmogony." In the same review (January 1, 1900), writing on "L'Idée de la Révélation," I said that revelation is not to be regarded "as the violent and unforeseen introduction of ready-made ideas into the human brain and intelligence."

In the same review (March 15, 1900), writing in an article termed "Les preuves et l'économie de la Révélation," I wrote that "miracle, properly understood, is the course of the world and life as viewed by faith, which alone penetrates the enigma; the same course of life and the world, viewed, as it were, from outside, by reason, becomes the order of nature, the domain of science and philosophy." As for prophecy, Scripture appears "as a great summary of religious hopes and aspirations, their birth and progress, and their partial and successive accomplishment; while their development and spiritualization, in spite of brutal checks from material events, constituted an admirable discipline of faith, and a non-negligible proof of the action of Providence in the history of religion."

Finally, in an article of the same review[1] (October 15, 1900), entitled "La Religion d'Israël, ses origines," I wrote that, "the chronological statements of the Bible," in regard to primitive epochs, "are now like a thin net cast like a bridge over an abyss of which we cannot see the bounds," and that "the first chapters of Genesis do not teach, nor seek to teach, under what circumstances man and religion made their entry into the world, nor what they were like in the prehistoric ages"; they only "give us to understand that man appeared on earth by the will and power of God, as

[1] *Revue du Clergé français.*

a creature, and that God watched over mankind in those distant ages as He has done later; and that He governed man with justice and mercy."

It was still saying a good deal. But the article was declared by Cardinal Richard, Archbishop of Paris, in a letter to the editor of the review (October 23, 1900) as being in contradiction with the Constitution *Dei Filius* of the Vatican Council, and with the encyclical *Providentissimus Deus*; and the publication of its continuation was forbidden.[1]

The rest of my *Essais d'histoire et de philosophie religieuses* was never published. But the chapters concerning the Gospel of Jesus and the institutional, doctrinal, and ritual development of Catholic Christianity are to be found in part in *L'Évangile et l'Église* which I wrote in 1902, by way of reply to the conferences of Harnack on the essence of Christianity (*Das Wesen des Christentums*, 1900), and in *Autour d'un petit livre*, written in 1903, in explanation of *L'Évangile et l'Église*: they were a sketch of Christian development, starting from the Gospel, and intended to show that the essence of the latter, if essence there were, had been truly perpetuated in Catholic Christianity, and that the transformations of the Gospel in Roman Catholicism had been something other than a progressive alteration. But my criticism of the Gospel, though cautious, was

[1] The sequel being already printed the whole was printed separately in a pamphlet *La Religion d'Israël* (1900), which was not at first put on sale. I brought out an augmented edition in 1908, and a third, completely recast, in 1933.

bolder on many points than that of Harnack; while my defence of the Roman Church implied an abandonment of the positive theses of scholastic theology regarding the formal institution of the Church and the sacraments by Christ, the immutability of dogma and the nature of ecclesiastical authority; of which authority I made an organ of human education, and not a power with absolute right over the intelligence and conscience of the faithful. This was why my apology for the Church was condemned as subversive of Catholic doctrine.

There followed a censure (inspired by Rome) of *L'Évangile et l'Église* by Cardinal Richard (January 17, 1903), to which seven other French prelates publicly adhered;[1] then a solemn condemnation of five of my works[2] by the Holy Office (December 16, 1903, with the approval of Pius X, December 17th) "as filled with very grave errors concerning primitive religion (this referred to *La Religion d'Israël*), the authenticity of Gospel facts and teaching, the divinity and the knowledge of Christ, the resurrection of Jesus,

[1] See the documents in appendix of *Autour d'un petit livre*.

[2] (a) *La Religion d'Israël* (pamphlet mentioned above). The Holy Office used it in support of the condemnation by Cardinal Richard in 1900; (b) *Études évangeliques*, published at the same time as *L'Évangile et l'Église* and containing a critical examination of the Gospel parables, with some commented fragments of the Fourth Gospel. (c) *L'Évangile et l'Église*. (d) *Autour d'un petit livre*. (e) *Le Quatrième Évangile*, a complete commentary of the Gospel of St. John, published in October 1903; when I presented this Gospel as a non-Apostolic work, allegorical, and a product of Christian mysticism.

the Divine institution of the Church and the Sacraments."[1]

Thus my attempt at historical reconstruction was interpreted as a collection of theological errors, and the ecclesiastical authority was next to demand of me to condemn it myself and to repudiate it under pain of being excommunicated by name.

The long and painful negotiations on which I then entered with the Archbishop of Paris, and with the Holy Office in the person of Cardinal Merry del Val, made me realize the true character of the Roman Church, and the vanity of my reforming apologetic. I was struck with major excommunication because I would only consent to a disciplinary submission, while reserving my opinions as an historian; whereas the authorities asked of me a complete disavowal of the condemned books and their contents.

The sentence, however, was suspended, in March 1904, because I had spontaneously renounced my work as free lecturer in the École pratique des Hautes Études, a post held since the end of 1900.[2] But the sense of profound fidelity which had kept me in the Church till then was quenched when it became evident to me that ecclesiastical authority demanded of me to

[1] This enumeration of errors is not in the Decree of the Holy Office, but in the letter which the Holy Office had charged Cardinal Merry del Val to write to Cardinal Richard in explanation of the Decree, see *Mémoires*, vol. ii, pp. 299–302.

[2] I do not know how the first-fruit of these lectures, *Les Mythes babyloniens et les premiers chapîtres le la Genèse*, which appeared in September 1901, escaped ecclesiastical censure.

serve it contrary to truth. In my retreat I continued my works of scientific exegesis, and my collaboration in the *Revue d'histoire et de littérature religieuses* and the *Revue critique*, and I completed the revision of my compared *Commentary of the Synoptic Gospels.*

When there followed the definite condemnation of Catholic Modernism in the decree *Lamentabili* of July 4, 1907, whose propositions had been largely drawn from *L'Évangile et l'Église* and *Autour d'un petit livre*, and in the Encyclical *Pascendi* of September 8, 1907, in which I was also touched, I was asked to subscribe to these pontifical pronouncements; I simply refused in letters dated January 12 and February 23, 1908; and excommunication by name was pronounced March 7, 1908.[1]

IV. TOWARDS A RELIGION OF MANKIND[2]

My spiritual and scientific liberty was henceforth free from all hindrance, and circumstances soon opened a new field. The Chair of the History of Religions had become vacant in the Collège de France, and I was called to it in March 1909. Up to then I had chiefly studied the Jewish religion and Christianity

---

[1] In the last years of January 1908 I had brought out *Les Évangiles Synoptiques* (two volumes) and *Simples Réflexions sur le Décret Lamentabili et l'Encyclique Pascendi*. In March 1908 I published *Quelques Lettres sur des questions actuelles et sur des événements récents*. Being condemned by Cardinal Richard (March 28, 1907) and by most French bishops the *Revue d'histoire et de littérature religieuses* suspended its publication at the beginning of 1908.

[2] See *Mémoires*, vol. iii, pp. 13–76.

in its origins; as also the ancient worships of Babylonia and Assyria.[1] I now had to place the Semitic religions in the whole frame of the religions of the world, to examine the essential elements of all religions, to analyse their character and form in the different cults, and thus to get at the intimate core of all religions and of religion.

These essential elements seemed to me to be sacrifice, divination, prophecy, prayer, and religious morality; and then the initiatives of reform whence sprang the religions termed universal, in opposition to national and tribal religions.

I began with sacrifice, for the rites of every religion are its most enduring element, that in which the spirit of each religion is best recognized; and sacrifice has been the first of all rites in ancient religions, if not also in Christianity. I wanted to study these matters in perfect freedom from all considerations of theological orthodoxy or scientific dogmatism. I could not expect to fulfil all the plan above indicated. In placing the great religious reformers at the end of my enumeration I did not oblige myself to speak of them, of those of first interest to us, Jesus and Paul, until I had exhausted the series of my themes as announced.

In my study of sacrifice, after having examined the rites of ancient religions, I was led to examine the

[1] Before publishing *Les Mythes babyloniens*, etc., I published in 1891-2 in the *Revue des Religions* an essay of popular character termed "Études sur la religion assyro-babylonienne," which seemed appropriate at that moment.

part of sacrifice in Christian worship; and this part showed itself under a very different light than when I examined Biblical texts and Christian origins in themselves, and not in their relation to the place in which they arose. If it were given to me to complete my research on sacrifice I intended to study anew the genesis of Christianity, the origin, quality and meaning of the New Testament writings, the metamorphosis of the Gospel into a mystery of Salvation, which was neither Judaism nor Paganism, but had drawn from both what was needed for its conquest of the Mediterranean world. The first results of my work were comprised in two volumes—*Essai historique sur le sacrifice,*[1] *Les Mystères païens et le mystère chrétien,*[2] and some other writings of less importance.[3]

And then the World War was to me a source of religious and moral experiences and impressions that completed my historical studies by demonstrating, in a peremptory manner, the powerlessness of existing forms of Christianity to realize that religion of universal brotherhood which was implied in the Gospel under the mythical notion of the reign of God.

[1] A *résumé* of the teaching given in 1909–16, published in 1920.

[2] Elaborated in 1912–13, published in a volume in 1919, after having appeared in chapters of the *Revue d'histoire et de littérature religieuses,* 1913–14. The review had reappeared in 1910, it suspended publication in 1915–19, to begin again in 1920–2. A second edition of *Mystères* appeared in 1930.

[3] *A propos d'histoire des religions* (1911); *L'Évangile selon S. Marc* (1912); and to the same series belongs the volume of *Choses passées,* an autobiographical essay, published in 1913.

Some have said that the war re-awoke religious faith in those who took part in it; but one would have to know to what religion they refer. There was, above all, an exaltation of nationalism, and the God of Christians, who is, rightly, the God of all mankind, found Himself reduced, almost everywhere, to the rank of a national god. It was, doubtless, because He had already taken that position, since the Gospel programme, not being realizable in itself, had more or less adapted itself to human conditions in seeking to mould them, while keeping its first character by placing the fulfilment of the kingdom of God in a future that could not be verified.

As I noted at that time, the religions regarded as universal, the religions of salvation, are rather "international confraternities of universalistic tendency. Christianity is one of these confraternities; it is a religion of the elect, not a truly universal religion; such a religion, based on the notion of humanity, does not yet exist."[1]

"All the ancient gods are inapt to the present crisis, yet there is a God implied in them whose formula must be found."[2]

"You cannot now satisfy peoples or individuals with tickets of immortality. Here I begin to glimpse the new God, who will be a greater human ideal, greater and truer than the Christ (of the Gospel);

[1] Note of February 7, 1915 (reproduced in the *Mémoires*, vol. iii, p. 303).
[2] Note of December 29, 1914 (*Mémoires*, vol. iii, p. 297).

even than the (transcendent) Christ of Paul, with his conception of personal sacrifice (immolation) as the ransom of sin; a conception which is inadequate, and must be replaced by simple devotion, unto death, to the ideal in view."[1]

"If there is to be a reign of justice—and we certainly desire it—let it be now. As we are not labouring in a *vacuum* our activity has eternal consequences; but whatever be those consequences, and whatever be the laws of the invisible world, this law of justice appears to us to be that of the visible world, the law of living humanity, and not the vague and uncertain hope of a dying humanity. . . . Gradually mankind forms itself a conscience; to some extent this conscience, within us, springs from the Gospel, was prepared thereby, and would not have been born without it—but it goes further."[2]

"The formation and direction of mankind must always contain a measure of mysticism, without which no true progress would be possible. The real dreamers are those pedants who imagine that the human animal can be perfected simply by a clear and reasoned knowledge of his material interests—a programme only for fools and beasts; if indeed it were possible to apply it in all rigour. If we cannot help seeing that religions have bequeathed us the mystery, rather than the meaning, of life and death, we do not therefore refuse all moral signification to either. We hope,

[1] Note of January 21, 1915 (*Mémoires*, vol. iii, p. 301).
[2] *Guerre et religion* (1915), 78–80.

on the contrary, to penetrate their moral value and meaning more fully."[1]

"The real difficulty is that the masses do not appreciate the inanity of the notion of an invisible, personal Being, whose business is to defend one against the enemy."[2]

At the beginning of the year 1917, in the midst of the horrors of the interminable war, I wrote my book on *Religion*. Whence arises in *mankind* the sense of humanity, and in *peoples* the appetite for mutual extermination?

"Far away voices of those who have gone before us, who are yet in and of us; voices near by, of our fallen brothers, who still speak though dead, and with more authority than if they were living; voice of our personal conscience, in which those other voices are echoed, they are those who speak the words to which we should listen. . . . The right place for meditation on life and death and duty is in the presence of life and death and duty, and not in the proud isolation of reason, which juggles with ideas in order to produce an artificial solution of the human problem. . . .

"Let us then face reality as it manifests itself in human history and in the present tragedy. Let us see: (1) what religion and morality have truly and humanly been in the history of man; (2) in what the great process of the religious and moral evolution of mankind has consisted, and whether morals have not always been

---

[1] *Mors et Vita* (1916), pp. 78–80.
[2] Note of April 9, 1915 (*Mémoires*, vol. iii, p. 318).

closely bound up with religion; (3) what have been the general factors and characters of this evolution, and whether it has not consisted in a progressive interiorization and individualization of religion and morals by the continued action of faith, tradition, will of sacrifice, and reason; (4) the part of human discipline in the efficacity of this evolution, a discipline embracing the lives of individuals, a discipline without which no society could be born or live; and the need of a more and more perfect discipline to assure the future of man and human civilization; (5) the manner in which that faith which upholds the moral life of man has been maintained—that is to say, by symbols, formulas, and rites, which have been the means of human communion as well as the source of religious emotion; and the question whether such symbols, which are fated to grow old, may not be susceptible of renewal without the death of that faith by which the just man lives."[1]

The object of the whole work was to show that a moral religion of humanity would be the crown of the religious and moral evolution of past ages.

"The religious revolution which has been at work in Europe for centuries, and to which is joined a political, social and scientific revolution of the Christian nations, has now reached a decisive moment. The actual war is not a mere quarrel of nations, it is a duel between humanity seeking to live and humanity not willing to die, between a religion in

---

[1] *La Religion* (first edition), pp. 34-7.

process of being and one in process of dying. . . . On
the issue of this tragic contest depends the fortune of
the future; a programme of betterment must be drawn
from this pit of misery and blood. The human vul-
tures who feed on this carnage must be denounced
for what they are—animal beings. The evangelical
ideal of human brotherhood must be raised again,
but with a truer sense of the conditions of life, and
our race must find other means of progress than
those of collective massacre. It was doubtless necessary
that humanity should suffer this paroxysm of madness,
hate, and cruelty in all its hideous force, that man might
rise therefrom to pursue with greater faith and energy
his ideal of wisdom, union, and goodness in all its
perfection."[1]

My considerations on *La Paix des nations et la
religion de l'avenir* (opening conference of my course
at the Collège de France, December 2, 1918) are
conceived in the same spirit.

"We are hoping that the world war will be succeeded
by the peace of nations, and it would seem as though
this universal peace should be the religion of the
future, since it is truly the religion of humanity."

And the following passages are quotations from the
same discourse.

"It will be to the everlasting honour of President
Wilson to have spoken the words that determined the
human meaning of the world war and the conditions
of human peace . . . a human peace guaranteed by

[1] *La Religion*, pp. 147–8.

a federation of nations, a union of all humanities in one humanity, a free and voluntary union of free nations desiring mutual justice. A new religion is thus authentically and solemnly promulgated, the first universal religion, because it is a religion of humanity, with a truly human ideal."

"The Society of Nations . . . such a society demands . . . human discipline, a discipline of religious morality such as has never yet existed on earth. Liberty must be subordinate to the service of mankind."

"This new humanity will demand stability and comfort, freedom of civilized progress; and all of these are inestimable goods . . . but the true human factor, which alone will uphold the Society of Nations and create the new humanity, is not reason or science, but the religious sentiment.

"The social instinct is always a principle of personal devotion and disinterestedness. This same instinct must therefore become, according to necessity, a principle of general human devotion and international disinterestedness. This example must, obviously, be set by such nations as have attained the highest human level.

"Christianity is our own human tradition; we can fill ourselves from it without entirely abandoning it. But Christianity itself is, willingly or unwillingly, in process of adaptation, and will probably fit itself more and more to the life of mankind.

"To the establishment of peace the aspirations

after justice, which have expressed themselves in Socialism, can make their contribution. . . . But if we look for an international fraternity by means of the Society of Nations, this does not legitimize international hatred through what is called class warfare.

"The great work before us can only be accomplished through faith and hope. Let us therefore draw from our ideal of humanity the strength that man has always found in faith. . . . The least task accomplished in a human spirit is a worthy contribution to the City of God. Do not let us think that the great interests of the world only concern our rulers . . . our leaders are helpless unless they are supported by the crowd. Little and great, we are one with one another, and unitedly responsible to mankind for what we do in the human interest."[1]

V. RELIGIONS AND RELIGION[2]

It may be thought that I regarded this religion of humanity only from the point of view of history, psychology, and morals, and that, if it implied a metaphysical and transcendental aspect, this was not indicated. This was because I did not care to shut religion into a philosophical system. Thus I wrote

[1] *La Paix des nations et la religion de l'avenir* (brochure, 1919), p. 6 and pp. 18, 23, 25, 28, 30.
I wrote at that time a little book *La Discipline intellectuelle*, a sequel to *La Religion*, which appeared in 1919.
[2] See *Mémoires*, vol. iii, pp. 377–562.

as follows to Fredrich von Hügel, on January 15, 1918, in regard to my work *La Religion:*

"I, too, know, on occasion, how to place myself in face of eternity, and I have no difficulty in realizing my littleness. I have in no way denied the existence of superhuman reality. I have felt the inadequacy of all speculation on the subject from the beginning until now. It is not exactly man's fault if he cannot see more clearly. Perhaps the wisest for him would be not to pretend to know that of which he is ignorant, and to accept his condition; which would be both easier and more profitable than to attempt to solve the problem of the universe by a disputed syllogism."[1]

Nothing could be truer. No religious philosophy, unless it be purely pragmatical, can establish itself save by marking its relation to a Supreme Being; I have tried to mark that relationship while avoiding the danger just indicated.

In this respect it will be enough to examine the series of my opening lectures at the Collège de France in 1919–26. That of December 1, 1919, "Du rôle et de l'avenir des sciences religieuses," ventures to claim, in the face of contemporary science, a chief position for religious science in the education of a new humanity, because "even historical science is not more conjectural than natural science," and because "the historical, psychological, and philosophical study of the religious and moral problem is an indispensable

[1] *Mémoires,* vol. iii, p. 352.

condition of the great effort which man must now make if he is not to degenerate."[1]

The problem is clearly defined in the Conference of December 4, 1920, on "L'illusion mystique et la vérité humaine":

"At the term of our study of sacrifice, beholding the immense illusions that this sacred action has perpetuated from century to century, and yet the moral and social advantages of which this institution, in itself without meaning and efficacity, has been the occasion, we may ask whether such be not the law of human progress: to buy a little truth by many illusions, a little morality by a more or less absurd discipline. The same question has pursued us throughout our examination of Christian origins. The deeper we carry our analysis of Christianity the more it would seem that Christianity has its source, not in a divine and incomprehensible fact, not in a simple moral experience, but in a sort of mystical and contagious vision, enfolded in a system as visionary as the faith it defends, and preserved in a literature of myths and fictions. Nevertheless, our personal experience and that of history tell us that Christianity has been and yet is a great religious and moral force. Let us endeavour to see more clearly whence proceeds this mystical illusion; why it was, not only inevitable, but even natural; and why, at the same time, it has always included an element of religious and moral truth that has grown while religions perished.

[1] *Religion et humanité* (Collection of Articles, 1926), pp. 73–80.

"Let us see, lastly, how this element of human mysticism and idealism, of which reason gives only a practical definition, would seem to be, in its origin and progress, an intuition, ever less and less imperfect, of a reality that presses upon us, of a life that urges us, of a human future and a world not yet made . . . of a mysterious and sacred power, in fact, that has been personified in ancestors, spirits, gods, and God . . . the power of the spirit, the soul of justice and goodness, the soul of humanity, working in society and in individuals, seeking ever fuller realization, and gradually succeeding in spite of many failures."[1]

In the lecture of December 1, 1923, on "Mysticism," I said:[2]

"Science as a whole, and in itself, is not a synthesis of definite results, but an indefinite programme of researches that will never be exhausted.

"Man's nature is deeper than his faculty of rational criticism, and it is from the depths of his nature that proceed, before any rudiment of methodical science, not only the need and desire to know, but in that very need and desire a mystical and spiritual sense, which is the basis of knowledge and the source of religion, morality, art, and true humanity. Mysticism, at its highest and simplest expression, is not a sensible vision nor the intellectual revelation of a super-terrestrial world; it is the intuitive apprehension of a

[1] *Religion et humanité*, pp. 135–6, 167.
[2] Printed as a preface to the second edition of *La Religion*, and resumed in *Religion et humanité*, pp. 28–41.

beyond that is present, of an infinitude in which my personal consciousness is momentarily absorbed in order to find itself again in a greater and better fullness and certitude. In the highest point of Christian mysticism, as in the Buddhist Nirvana, we find the spirit of human disinterestedness and devotion; the liberation from mere animality, from sensuality and selfishness."[1]

The lecture of December 9, 1934, "De l'Esprit,"[2] seeks to show that the absolute distinction between spirit and matter is not as plain to us as it was to the ancients, and that the infinite aspect and intimate character of universal reality outstrips the reach of our minds.

The conclusion was as follows:

"It is much less important to speculate on the nature of the spirit . . . than to carry on the work of the spirit, to contribute to its coming and participate in it. . . . This is why the service of the spirit is one with the religion of humanity."[3]

In the lecture of December 5, 1935, "De la Foi,"[4] faith is declared to be "a normal form of the mystical sense, and an essential element of the life of the spirit."

Further on:

"It is no paradox to maintain that theological theories do not express the true psychology of faith; and thus one may partly understand, though not excuse, the contemptuous indifference to faith of

[1] *La Religion* (2nd edition), pp. 25–48–37.
[2] Reproduced in *Religion et humanité*, pp. 172–98.
[3] *Religion et humanité*, pp. 197–8.
[4] Reproduced in *Religion et humanité*, pp. 199–229.

many contemporary savants. The theories in question are not so much an analysis of living faith as an apology for belief, or the system of belief in which faith is defined in the various religious groups. For there is no faith without belief, but neither is belief faith; faith is, properly speaking, a sentiment of trust in the object that belief endeavours to define.

"Scholastic theologians have been, and are, in great part, very arrogant reasoners; they have a family likeness to the scientific and rational dogmatists, who have as mythical a conception of reason and science as theologians of revelation."

"The harmony of reason and faith is a fictitious problem, because it is only reason, whether theological or scientific, that creates absolute dogmas, which it wrongly imposes on itself. . . . The true, real, and permanent problem is, through all the evolutions of personal and general culture, through all the accidents of life and the little and great crises of civilization, to assure the stability of the mind and conscience of humanity in its social and international relations, in its quest of social and moral perfection. It is not science that can suffice to secure this stability, which can never be wholly perfect. . . . We need faith . . . and faith has never been anything else than a firm adherence to the life of the spirit. It is faith which is a profound sense of reality and a vision of the ideal, that urges on religion, science, morality and art to ever new progress."[1]

[1] *Religion et humanité*, pp. 199, 219-27.

In pursuance of this same effort at defining the human problem I brought out in 1923 a little book entitled *La Morale humaine* (re-edited in 1928), which treats at bottom of the same problem, but from the practical point of view, and which aims at defining the religious ideal in the order of education and of the discipline demanded by a religion of humanity. I will quote its following concluding lines:

"There is no greater love than that which gives its life for the loved ones. This gift of self is the fulfilment of man, it is the end of every discipline, the condition of every society, whether domestic, civil, or human, the law of all true humanity. The most difficult thing and the most necessary is not, perhaps, that which has hitherto been regarded as the most glorious. . . . This ordinary sacrifice, which is indispensable to the common life of society . . . will always be the daily bread of social life; it will not cease to be necessary even when nations shall have renounced the absurdity, the abomination, the inhumanity of war. It is by the continuity, the perfection and the increasing spontaneity of sacrifice that humanity will be upheld; and it is by the exercise of this love and devotion that mankind will find peace, consolation, and happiness.

"Sacrifice will consolidate all the joys that life can offer because it will crown them with love. And thus human morality will end by creating humanity itself."[1]

[1] *La Morale humaine*, pp. 291–2 (second edition, pp. 298–9). To omit nothing I will mention also a brief incursion into religious politics, *L'Église et la France*, 1925.

My exegetical work, resumed in 1916, in connection with my teaching at the Collège de France, until 1926, was actively pursued during this period,[1] so as to prepare those essays of synthesis which I published during the last years.[2] In all this I sought to throw light on the problem of Christian origins, and this research helped me greatly in the elaboration of what I will venture to call my religious philosophy, in which I endeavoured to determine the human value of Christianity. If certain ones of my critical conclusions have appeared to some minds subversive of Christianity it is perhaps because they have not taken sufficient count of their relation to this further end.

For the time has now come to conclude by noting the place that Christianity occupies in the scale of human values when we take count of the development of natural science in these later times; of our present knowledge of the universe, of our human and pre-

[1] L'Épitre aux Galates (1916); Les Actes des Apôtres (1920); Le Quatrième Évangile, second edition (1921); Les Livres du Nouveau Testament, translated from Greek into French, with a general introduction and notices (1922); L'Apocalypse de Jean (1923); L'Évangile selon Luc (1924). Some parts of my course were published in the Revue d'histoire et de littérature religieuses in 1920— thus Les premières années du Christianisme (opening conference, December 1, 1917); La littérature du Christianisme primitif, La Carrière de l'Apôtre Paul (1921); Les Épitres de Paul, Les Épitres attribuées à Paul et les Épitres Catholiques, La Didaché et les lettres des Pères apostoliques (1922); De la méthode en histoire des religions (opening conference, December 3, 1921); L'Apocalyptiqu chrétienne, La Légende de Jésus (1922).

[2] La Religion d'Israël (third edition, 1933); La Naissance du Christianisme (1933); Le Mandéisme et les origines chrétiennes (1934).

historic science, of human paleontology, of prehistoric and historic archaeology. One cannot too earnestly urge theologians of all Christian Churches and believers of all the religions of the world to contemplate the infinite perspectives that are unfolded before us on every side, and before which mythology and theology, even the most ancient, fade like a dream. Let them consider the immensity of the universe that is revealed to us, with the unfathomable harmony of its laws; the formerly unsuspected mystery of the innumerable worlds, and the equally ignored mystery of the atom and of the infinitely little. Of all the ancient cosmogonies nothing remains.

Certainly the mystery of the world does not eliminate the mystery of God, but it singularly intensifies and transposes it. What becomes of the idea of creation save as a symbol of ancient magic? And who would now be so mad as to count the years of the world? The ancients ignored the unfathomable depth of the mystery of the world and of God; and this fact is of importance in itself and in its consequences. And in their sacred books the mystery of man was equally ignored. The slow and painful ascension of this being from animality to a progressive consciousness of his humanity, through the incalculable millenaries of pre-history, is beginning to dawn upon us, and the origins of history itself show themselves under a new light, beginning from the history of that Near East where the religion of Israel and Christianity arose. Of this last mystery our Bible knows hardly anything; Israel and his God, who has become the God of the Christians, come late into the history of man and of the Mediterranean East. Its sacred legend, because it is a legend, and because it is comparatively recent in its traditional form, adjusts itself badly to the history which is gradually being constituted of the second millenary before the Christian era and the two previous millenaries; even the sacred legend of Christianity, contained in the New Testament, has but a slight relation to history.[1] Of this second fact we may well say that it is of importance in itself and in its consequences. The principal consequence to be deduced from this double fact may be expressed in a few words: The Jewish and the Christian religion do not constitute a primordial, unique, and definite fact in the religious evolution of mankind; they are a product, remarkable, and even the most remarkable, of that historic evolution.

This is not to say that we need therefore despair of the future of religion on our planet. The Christian ideal was never more necessary nor more opportune than in the present movement of civilization. As I wrote in 1934:

"The Christian ideal expresses itself in three ways:

1. In the notion of a reign of justice, realized or to be realized, by the law of charity, although, if one may dare say so, the Gospel, in virtue of its eschatological

[1] On this point see *La Naissance du christianisme*, pp. 46–61, and in *Le Mandéisme et les origines chrétiennes*, the appendix "Le Problème des origines chrétiennes" (opening conference of December 5, 1931).

character, expresses this message in an Utopian form, and imperfectly.

2. In the notion of an interior peace which man gains by his confidence and faith in the regeneration of his soul under the reign of justice and love—although the regeneration in question, as presented in the childishly mythological system of the Epistles, is as arbitrary and inconsistent a gnosis as those termed heretical.

3. In the notion of a universal society of believers, of the Catholic Church as the *patria* of souls united in the practice of justice through the law of love, and in the confidence inspired by the sentiment of regeneration under this sublime law—although traditional Catholicism, with its imposed orthodoxy, its autocratic hierarchy, its blindly imperialistic papacy, seems, in many ways, a caricature of the ideal Catholicity that it claims to represent.

"Thus the Christian ideal might be regarded as the essence of Christianity, imperfectly realized in historical Christianity; and it might be also the essence of the religion of humanity, indefinitely realizable in the future."[1]

Just as ancient Christianity, by adapting itself to the conditions of the Mediterranean world, conquered it, by introducing a principle of human life superior

[1] See note "La Valeur humaine du Christianisme," published in *Revue de métaphysique et de morale*, October 1934. Compare also *Y a-t-il deux sources de la Religion et de la Morale*, first edition, 1933, second edition, 1934 (being a criticism of the work of M. Bergson, *Les Deux Sources de la Morale et de la Religion*).

to all the pagan religions and to Greek wisdom, so let those who uphold the same ideal, though stripped of its traditional entanglements, and enlarged to meet contemporary needs and aspirations, raise their minds to the height of all true knowledge. Let them open their eyes to the light that comes from every side; and their hearts to the travail and labour of mankind; that they may infuse into that labour the divine principle of love and devotion; and may a religion be realized on earth that shall be the crown of Christianity and all other religions, and that shall perfect all men and lead them into the life of the spirit and of communion with God.

BIBLIOGRAPHY

Liste des publications l'auteur, anciennes et récentes, actuellement à la librairie Émile Nourry, Paris:

Études bibliques. 3e édition, 1903.

L'Évangile et l'Église. 5e édition, 1930.

Simples réflexions sur le décret du Saint Office Lamentabili sane exitu et sur l'Encyclique Pascendi Dominici Gregis. 2e édition, 1908.

Quelques lettres sur des questions actuelles et sur des événements récents. 1908.

Leçon d'ouverture du cours d'histoire des religions au Collège de France. 1909.

A propos d'histoire des religions. 1911.

Choses passées. 1913.

Mors et Vita. 2e édition, 1917.

La Paix des nations et la religion de l'avenir. 1919.

La Religion. 2e édition, 1924.

De la discipline intellectuelle. 1919.

Les Mystères païens et le mystère chrétien. 2ᵉ édition, 1930.

Essai historique sur le Sacrifice. 1920.

Les Livres du Nouveau Testament, traduits du grec en français, avec introduction générale et notices. 1922.

La Morale humaine. 2e édition, 1928.

L'Évangile selon Marc. 1912.

L'Évangile selon Luc. 1924.

Le Quatrième Évangile. 2ᵉ édition, 1921.

Les Actes des Apôtres 1920.

L'Épitre aux Galates. 1916.

L'Apocalypse de Jean. 1923.

L'Église et la France. 1925.

Religion et humanité. 1926.

Mémoires pour servir à l'histoire religieuse de notre temps. 1931.

Y a-t-il deux sources de la religion et de la morale? 2ᵉ édition, 1934.

La Religion d'Israël. 3ᵉ édition. 1933.

La Naissance du Christianisme. 1933.

Le Mandéisme et les origines chrétiennes. 1934.

Remarques sur la littérature épistolaire du Nouveau Testament. 1936.

Les Origines du Nouveau Testament. 1936.

George Tyrrell et Henri Bremond. 1936.

A la même librairie, collection de la *Revue d'histoire et de littérature religieuses*, années 1910–14, 1920–2.

The Making of a Psychologist of Religion

JAMES H. LEUBA[1]

Professor Emeritus of Psychology, Bryn Mawr College, Pennsylvania

I PROPOSE to put down here what I know of the influences which have shaped the course of my life so as to make me devote whatever time I could spare from my duties as professor of psychology in an American college to the understanding of the experiences commonly called "religious."

A career is, of course, never determined exclusively by one's inborn inclinations and abilities. Social influences play their powerful role in moulding one's opinions, interests, and purposes. Opportunity —chance as we say—does the rest and one finds oneself treading, often for life, a particular route. My case was, I think, the usual one for persons with a mental endowment of a somewhat definite sort. I waited, as it were, for opportunities promising some degree of satisfaction to my dominant interests. My impression is that, in the choice of a career, Fortune has not been unkind to me. I must add, however, that at several junctures, before I found my way to

[1] Professor Leuba married in 1896. He is father of two children, a boy and a girl. The son, Clarence, is Professor of Psychology at Antioch College, Ohio; and the daughter, Gladys, teaches dramatics and diction.

Clark University as scholar in psychology, the necessity of making a living came very near launching me in a very different direction than the one I have followed. I still recoil in dread at the thought of the misfit I might have become.

In his early life my father was a watchmaker; later, he became a watch manufacturer in the distinguished little town of Neuchâtel in French Switzerland. When, during the second half of the last century, great watch manufactures were set up in the United States and brought ruin to the dominant industry of a large part of Switzerland, my father conceived the project of invading the enemy's country to seek there a livelihood for his large family. It was at that time, for a man in his circumstances, a very bold project, and our first years in America were difficult and lean years indeed.

My first pressing task was to learn English. I had just received the Bachelor's degree from the University of Neuchâtel, the institution from which the famous Agassiz and Guyot came to the United States in 1848. Good luck led me to a small Pennsylvania college where I was induced to join the senior class while earning my living by sweeping classrooms and tending stove fires. Somebody, interested in the establishment of a French branch of the New York Y.M.C.A., discovered me there and I was induced to become its secretary. I remained two years in that position. Why I left it, I shall say later on. My next occupation was that of teacher of French and German in a reputed New England preparatory school. While there, I heard that Clark University was offering a number of scholarships and I was fortunate enough to secure one of them to study psychology under G. Stanley Hall and Edmund Sanford, two pioneers of the new science. I had found my way.

But why not remain a teacher of languages? For the very good reason that I had absolutely no taste and hardly any respect for that occupation. And why select psychology among the sciences? To answer that question and explain why the psychology of religion became a life-long interest, I must go back to my life at Neuchâtel. It will be seen that the selection of psychology as a career was not altogether haphazard, for the most impressive experiences of my youth had made me unusually curious about human nature.

My parents were earnest Church members. There was, however, in my father a critical attitude and a curiosity sufficient to have made of him a downright heretic had he possessed enough knowledge. He looked sympathetically into several religious movements with which he happened to come in contact, in search, it seemed to me, of a simpler religion, less theological and more practical. In any case, I did not learn from him implicit obedience to established authority.

It was the custom at Neuchâtel for young men who had reached adolescence to undergo an intensive religious instruction, lasting through several months, in preparation for their first Communion and the ratification of the vows made in their behalf, by their parents, at the baptismal ceremony. The pastor under whose instruction I came was a member of the famous Godet family, the son of Frederick Godet, the New Testament scholar. My state of mind during that period is well described by the expression "puzzled misery." It was not so much the fault of the pastor —a good and intelligent man—but that of the religion he faithfully taught us: a mitigated Calvinism, as I remember it. We had to learn by heart and profess belief in the catechism and in at least one creed. The Ten Commandments gave me no trouble, I felt their value and accepted them wholeheartedly. But the creed and catechism appeared to me so strange, so remote from what I could understand, and practically so irrevelant or worse, that they left me reticent and chilled. Why demand of me an affirmation of belief in these doctrines? The authority of the Church by which they were presented, backed, as I was told, by God Himself, awed me, but did not produce faith. And yet I was not able to formulate any sufficient reason for standing up against my teacher and the Church and say, "I do not believe." In puzzled misery I went up to my first Holy Communion and took upon myself the vows made in my behalf at baptism. But entrance into full Church membership evoked no moral enthusiasm. Whatever social passion could have been awakened in me by the Gospels had been smothered by fantastic, incomprehensible doctrines; and—horrible indeed—I had been taught that without these doctrines, which touched none of the springs of life in me, there was no salvation for me or humanity! There was obviously something wrong with me, or was it with religion? I did not know; I did not even clearly formulate these questions.

The second powerful and altogether different religious experience of my life came with the arrival of the Salvation Army to my home town. General Booth was beginning to send his crusaders over the Continent. Their reception at Neuchâtel was marked by an outburst of religious intolerance incredible in a country which justly boasts of an old tradition of religious and political freedom. The poor Salvationists were insulted, stoned, and finally thrown into jail. My father sided with those who demanded religious freedom and joined some citizens to form a guard for the officers of the Army as they went to and from their meetings. Blows were exchanged. As to the police, they declared themselves unable to keep the peace. The whole canton was in commotion, and, at one time, the Federal authorities held troops in readiness to remedy the supineness of the State police.

Now that the Salvation Army has gained a foothold all over the world and is regarded generally as a useful social agency, it is difficult to understand fully what brought to red heat the irritation of that Swiss population. The main cause was probably the aggressive arrogance of a handful of foreigners

M

who truculently and in bad French admonished the Christian population of smug Neuchâtel to repent their sins, believe in the Lord Jesus Christ and be saved. The attitude of the Church people and of the clergy in this occurrence was not one to recommend them to me.

Drawn into these stirring events I attended the meetings of the Army and came to know several of its leaders. Their courage and uncompromising devotion to a moral ideal captured my admiration. They talked a great deal, it is true, of the blood of Christ, of the Cross, of Heaven and Hell, but for me these beliefs were thrown into the background by the life of the loud-mouthed, tactless heroes who urged them. The moment came when I could no longer resist the appeal of the moral ideal they were for ever holding up before us: no compromise with evil, no half-way measure, no divided self; every impurity had to be disavowed, the divine Will alone was to rule.

In the conversion through which I passed, the doctrinal background, presented so vividly and tirelessly by my friends of the Army, played a remarkably small role. It is the moral ideal itself which moved me. I saw it as an Absolute which it was my duty and privilege to realize. There was, in addition, an acute sense of guilt for having fallen short of a perfection regarded as attainable. This ethico-religious experience was perhaps the most beneficial one of my life; it was certainly the most violent one. But,

I repeat, in spite of the vociferous affirmations of my religious friends, I did not feel that belief in the atoning sacrifice of Christ was a condition of salvation; the forces working in me had no vital relation to that doctrine.

After a few months of strife, peace returned and the Salvationists were allowed to go on unmolested with their campaign for the salvation of Neuchâtel. As to me, I found myself engrossed more and more in studies for the degree of Bachelor of Science and gradually ceased to have much to do with the Salvation Army. I retained, however, until my departure for America, my connection with the Y.M.C.A. My scientific studies had doubtless a profound influence upon me, unfavourable to the traditional theology, but it worked so gradually that I was hardly aware of its effects. We were driven so hard that there was very little time for us students to read and think outside of the prescribed courses. I made time, however, to read Darwin and Huxley, and found in the theory of evolution, then fighting for recognition, explanatory ideas which seemed to me fundamental. The sciences to which I was being introduced, physics, chemistry, geology, biology, presented a method for finding the truth, and pointed to a world view so completely different from the method and the conception of the pious people among whom I had moved, that I felt keenly the contrast. With regard to the "truths," preached by the Churches, which appeared to me in direct contradiction with

Darwinism and science in general, I found myself siding without hesitation with science.

By the time I had reached the United States much of religion, as it had been taught me, had been set aside. How much remained I would have found it difficult to say; enough in any case to make it possible for me, a year later, to accept the General Secretaryship of the French Y.M.C.A. in New York. I laboured there two years and found much satisfaction in helping young men to live honestly and happily, and to make their way in the great metropolis. But the prayer-meetings became more and more a burden to me, and the moment came when I could no longer go on with the strictly religious part of the activities I was expected to lead. I resigned to the great relief both of the zealots among the directors and of myself.

When, after a year of French and German teaching, I heard that there was a strong department of psychology at Clark University and that students were helped with scholarships and fellowships, I saw my opportunity. The physical and the biological sciences were throwing a wonderful light upon the mysteries of the world, but what I wanted to understand above all was the working of the human mind. Psychology, thought I, would in particular clear up, among other things, the wonders of conversion and of the religious life in general.

When, two years later, I had to choose a topic for a doctor's dissertation, I did not hesitate. No topic had been so interesting and important to me as Christian conversion. President Hall was not encouraging. Did he think that the subject was beyond me? I do not know. Ultimately, as I was insistent and confident, he blessed my undertaking with a phrase characteristic of the great teacher he was.

My dissertation, published in 1896, in the *American Journal of Psychology* (vol. vii), under the title "Studies in the Psychology of Religious Phenomena—Conversion," was, I think, the first attempt to submit an important religious experience to scientific treatment in the light of contemporary psychology. It consisted mainly of an analysis and explanation of a large number of Christian conversions, many of them secured by the author himself in interviews with the converts. In this attempt was implied the opinion that there was no difference of kind between religious and non-religious consciousness and that the religious truths were to be based, like any other, on scientific knowledge.

In the following volume of the same journal (vol. viii) Edwin Starbuck came out with "A study of Conversion"; and in 1899 appeared his well-known book, *The Psychology of Religion*. In 1902 the brilliant work of William James, *The Varieties of Religious Experience*, brought into some prominence the earlier work of the two young pioneers.

My work for the doctor's degree was not yet entirely completed when President Hall offered to recommend me for a vacant position at Wesleyan University. He informed me, incidentally, that I would have to take turns with the faculty members in leading chapel. I protested that I could not do that. To my great astonishment I was told that if I would not conform to the customs of the land I would not get along. Dr. Hall was regarded in the town as in good religious standing, but those who associated with him intimately were better informed. The discovery of how widespread among men of influence was the attitude represented by the President of Clark University was one of the painful experiences of my early manhood. It has not been without influence in sustaining my efforts not only to seek the truth but to spread it as widely as I might.

I have never forgotten the attempt, when I was at the French Y.M.C.A., of a worthy clergyman to load the scales of evidence with the prestige and authority of great names. This happened at the height of a harassing struggle with the doctrine of the atonement, which he and others were trying to force upon me. Among the persons mentioned to me as that of believers in the atonement doctrine was Alexandre Vinet, a distinguished Swiss theologian and littérateur, for whom I had great admiration. A little later I chanced upon one of his letters to a friend in which he confessed to perplexity, not regarding the doctrine, but concerning the public stand he should take. Should he unsettle the convictions of the young by admitting his own unbelief? To scrupulous men, the problem may come in that form. In the mind of numberless others it assumes less worthy aspects. But, whatever reasons those in position of influence give to themselves for appearing to hold religious views which they reject, the effect of that practice upon the young, who struggle to build up a system of belief by which they may live, amounts to the presentation of false evidences, and results in the harmful prolongation of obsolete traditions.

As a result of my refusal to go to Wesleyan University I remained two years longer in Worcester engaged in psychological researches at the university and in earning a living by giving lectures in the town, on psychology and French literature. When, in 1897, I secured an appointment at Bryn Mawr College to organize a department of psychology, it was with the understanding, at my request, that I would begin a year later, after a journey abroad. The year (1897–8) was spent in getting acquainted with the work of the leading psychologists and educators in German and French universities.

During that journey my interest in the psychology of religion remained in abeyance, as also during my first years at Bryn Mawr. As soon, however, as I could make some leisure I returned to my favourite subject of research. My interest in the psychology of religious life has continued unabated to this day.

The full significance of the entrance of scientific psychology in the field of religious experience did not, of course, appear to me immediately. I was aware, however, that only the methods of the historian and of the literary critic had been brought to bear upon the religions. These methods are applied to the external manifestations of religion; the beliefs and practices, historical development, mutual relationships, date and authorship of the sacred books, etc. Much will doubtless still be added to our knowledge by the historian and the literary critic but the main conclusions to which their methods of research can lead have been obtained, their essential work is done.

The psychology of religion, on the other hand, is concerned with the experiences themselves out of which come beliefs, practices, and institutions. It enters the very heart of religious life which, it was said, could be examined from the outside but never entered by science. To make of religious experience a field open to psychology, without reservation, *on exactly the same terms and with the same expectations* as any other part of human experience, constituted a momentous departure. It implied the setting aside of the claim of religion to a unique, superhuman nature.

The demarcation of the field I intended to cover by the term "religion" constituted a preliminary problem. It appeared to me that the only clear way of separating the religions from the rest of life was not by their end, but by the method or means they use to reach their end. That method is appealed to, and reliance upon superhuman beings. In that way, and in that way only, can the institutions which have been and are, by common consent, called religions be differentiated from magic, from purely ethical systems like Confucianism and ethical culture societies, and from all other forms of "humanism." I was aware of the strong tendency to use "religion" in a sense so broad and vague that the distinctive feature I have pointed out is lost sight of, so that it becomes practically impossible to separate religion from any activity of great importance to the welfare of humanity. But whether or not it be desirable so to use the term, my interest was in religion as defined above.

It seemed, therefore, logical to begin the rather comprehensive and systematic study I had in mind with the psychological origin, the development and the function of the god-conceptions. As belief in continuation after death is almost everywhere intimately connected with religion, I added immortality to my primary subject of inquiry. And so it came to pass that the first part of my first book (*A Psychological Study of Religion*, 1912) treats of the origin, early development, and function of the god-ideas; and the first part of the second (*The Belief in God and Immortality*, 1916) takes up the same topics with reference to immortality.

The preparation of the first of these books involved the consideration of the relation of magic to religion, and led to a clear separation of those two forms of behaviour so generally left insufficiently differentiated by students of early religion. Magic and religion have, undoubtedly, much in common; their aim and their gross results are often identical, and they are both steeped in awe and mystery. They differ, radically, however, by their method. At times, the non-civilized enters into social relations with invisible beings in order to placate them or win their assistance; he begs from them, he offers presents, he praises and promises obedience—that is religion. At other times, or even simultaneously and for the same purpose, he uses non-social means of action upon spirits, gods, men, or things; he makes, for instance, an effigy and does to it what he would like to happen to the object or person represented; he eats the fat of a courageous animal in the expectation of becoming courageous himself; he secures the name of the god and, by the power that is in the name, he compels the god to do his will—that is magic. The presence or absence of a personal social relationship constitutes an undeniably definite and important difference. Moreover, this meaning of the terms "religion" and "magic" corresponds with common usage.

The most important and far-reaching generalization arising from a study of origins is that belief both in superhuman, personal agents and in continuation after death proceeds from two altogether different sources: the irrepressible habit to explain by assigning causes, and the equally irrepressible habit of seeking help in the struggle for life.[1] If these two sources

[1] The habit to understand, to assign causes, is formed because of its value in the struggle for life. Nevertheless, very soon it seems to exist for its own sake.

led, on the one hand, to identical conceptions of gods and, on the other, to identical conceptions of immortality, nothing more would have to be said about it. But it is quite otherwise. The god-conceptions arising as causal explanations of natural phenomena possess the attributes necessary to produce these phenomena; these attributes, however, need not be those required in order to provide the help wanted by man at any particular moment. The sun god, for instance, is competent to produce heat and light, but need not possess the power to assist his worshippers in their struggles with enemies.

The explanatory conceptions of gods are, however, soon supplemented or altered. Under the pressure of his need for help, man adds to them the desirable qualities and powers which he himself lacks, so that they may be able to gratify every one of his desires.

Thus, by objectifying his ideals in gods, originally due to an effort to explain striking experiences, and in entering into social relations with them, man actually accomplishes the miracle of lifting himself up by his boot-straps: he gets from his relation with gods something at least of the wealth with which he has endowed them.

In the double origin of the god-conceptions lurks, unfortunately, an element of conflict. Insignificant at first, it becomes the deadly conflict of science or, as one should rather say, of philosophy with religion. The crude, primitive explanations in terms of personal, superhuman beings, are replaced in science and most philosophies by impersonal forces. The universe is conceived as an infinite, impassive Absolute—a conception destructive of the kind of god who can enter into social relation with man. It makes impossible belief in a heavenly Father able and ready to comfort and succour. This conflict of the "heart" with the "head" is the main cause of the confusion and contentions which have characterized the relation of religion with science and philosophy.

The same two sources appear even more clearly in connection with immortality. The original belief in continuation after death—I have called it the Primary belief—arose as an unavoidable explanation of certain pseudo-perceptions such as the apparition, in dreams and other visions, of persons who had died. Survival was for the primitive a fact as evident as the existence of the external world: he saw, heard, felt the ghosts. Desire for survival had no share in the production of the belief.

As a matter of fact, man was not at first concerned about his own survival, but he was very much concerned about the ghosts of others. The thought of their proximity, even of the ghosts of his friends, made him uneasy, and his chief desire was that they should go away and let him alone. Primary survival involved, therefore, neither reward nor punishment for deeds performed on earth; and, as to paradises, the thought of them developed slowly and was of short duration in so far as the Primary belief is concerned. Before the Christian era, among the populations from which came European civilization, the belief in survival after death had become, for reasons too long to be recounted here, a dreadful perspective. Babylonians, Egyptians, Hebrews, and Greeks agreed in the depressive pictures they drew of the life of the shades in the Other World.

It is under these circumstances that, in these lands, the yearnings of the heart, which had been transforming the conceptions of the divine beings, came to fruition in this sphere also, and produced the modern conception of immortality. The failure of justice on earth, the ending at death of affection, love, personality—things to which man had learned to attach supreme value—seemed so irrational as to be an impossibility. The desire for their preservation and fulfilment was intense enough to father a belief in a future life which would give it satisfaction. Under the influence of Christ's life and death, the conception in process of formation acquired the well-known features of the Christian doctrine of immortality. It became a source of moral strength and happiness. Here again man managed to lift himself up by his own boot-straps.

The separation of these two kinds of continuation after death, the Primary and the Modern, with their different psychological origin and function, seems to me an important feature of "The Belief in God and Immortality."

A lively interest in the contemporary status of the Christian religion manifested itself in the inclusion in these first two books of a discussion of two problems of actuality. In *A Psychological Study of Religion*, a long chapter (pp. 207–80) was devoted to the demonstration that, under the pressure of philosophical criticism, the modern Protestant leaders have ceased to rely upon the traditional metaphysical proofs of the existence of God, and that they regard "religious experience" as the one assured ground of belief. In effecting that retreat, they thought that they were placing the fundamental religious beliefs outside the realm of science and philosophy, i.e. in an altogether unassailable position; for they imagined that religious experience provides a direct, immediate knowledge of God, i.e., a knowledge independent of the natural ways of securing knowledge. As a matter of fact, if by that move they escaped from the destructive historical critics, geologists, and biologists, they placed themselves completely in the hands of the psychologists. Religious experience is obviously a part of the field of psychology. The discovery of the forces that work in religious life and of the conditions under which they act are psycho-physiological problems. Without realizing it, the theologians of inner experience introduced the enemy into the citadel itself. They brought down the "divine truths," based on inner experience, to the level of the hypotheses formed to explain any other part of experience.

In Part II of *The Belief in God and Immortality* was introduced a statistical study of the religious beliefs of the persons listed in Cattell's directory, *American*

Men of Science (edition of 1910). They were tabulated in four classes: physical scientists, biological scientists, sociologists, and psychologists; and each class was divided into a more and a less distinguished group. For the first time we had a reliable knowledge of the proportions of believers and disbelievers in the god of the religions and in personal immortality among all American men of science.

The inquiry was repeated in the same way, in 1933. Thus, definite knowledge of the movement of belief among scientists was provided.[1]

Although the Christian circle among whom I was brought up did not call themselves mystics, the religious life with which I was acquainted in my youth was far from devoid of mysticism, if one understands by that term a condition taken to be a union or communion of the individual with God. Whether William James's opinion, that mysticism is the essence of all religious life, be true or not, it would be difficult to point to any religion, high or low, where practices designed to place man in contact with a superhuman world did not exist.

The extraordinary delightfulness of the mystical experience, its vivifying effects, and the mysterious superhuman knowledge which it is supposed to

---

[1] A brief summary of that second inquiry, together with a comparison of its results with those of the first, have been published in *Harper's Magazine* for August 1934. I might add that I have now almost concluded a comparable research among four other classes of people, as they are listed in *Who's Who in America*: bankers, other business people, lawyers, and writers.

reveal, make of it a particularly fascinating subject of inquiry for the psychologist. *The Psychology of Religious Mysticism* (International Library of Psychology, Philosophy, and Scientific Method, Kegan Paul, Trench, Trübner & Co., London, and Harcourt, Brace & Co., New York, 1925) was the product of long years of study, the first fruit of which had appeared many years earlier in two extensive articles under the title, "Les Tendances fondamentales des mystiques chrétiens" (*Revue philosophique*, Paris, 1902, pp. 1–36; 441–87).

I approached mysticism as I had the notion of gods and of immortality, i.e., I looked for its original manifestations in early societies and for the main lines of its development. I made an inductive study based upon the careful, comparative examination, in the light of contemporary psychology, of a large number of various experiences called "mystical," taken without as well as within the sphere of religion.

Mystical practices giving entrance to a mysterious superhuman world are no more prerogatives of the civilized than the beliefs in gods and in continuation after death. At first, drugs are used to produce the mystical state; later on, they are replaced by various bodily and mental movements and attitudes. Among us it is produced by the bodily and mental attitudes characteristic of the various "degrees of prayer," as the Christian mystics say. *The Psychology of Religious Mysticism* begins, accordingly, with chapters on drug-intoxication and mysticism, and follows up with a detailed account of the experiences described by great Christian mystics.

The divine Presence and the communication of superhuman knowledge are the two distinctive claims made by the mystics. They constitute outstanding problems for the psychologist. A large part of the book is, therefore, given up to a study, partly experimental, of the "sense of divine Presence" and of the nature of mystical knowledge. That knowledge is held by the mystic to be neither an inference from sensory and affective data, nor a deduction from general propositions, but something immediately apprehended, given. It is, therefore, considered as inaccessible to science and altogether unassailable.

In this claim the mystic is in error. His assurance of the presence of God has the same kind of origin as that of the assurance of the non-civilized who, when he hears the thunder, thinks he is aware of the thunder-god. What he really hears is a peculiar sound, and from it he *infers* the existence of a great being who produces the sound. Similarly, the mystic experiences a mass of more or less unusual sensations, feelings, emotions, and concludes that they are a divine manifestation. Both, unaware of the inference they have made, think they are in possession of direct, "immediate" knowledge. As a matter of fact, their knowledge is an inference. Whether it be correct or not, is to be determined, as in the case of other inferences, by scientific and philosophical considerations. The complete assurance they have that they are right is, of

N

course, in itself, in no way a proof of rightness. A mistaken absolute certainty is not a rare occurrence.

But although the prayer of communion and the higher degrees of the "mystical ascent to God" are not what the mystic imagines, they may have, nevertheless, in addition to the delight they procure, a very definite moral value. The source of that value is the subject of a chapter of my last book.

While engaged in the work just sketched, I had endeavoured to maintain the purely scientific attitude of the dispassionate inquirer. I cannot, however, pretend that I had ceased to be interested in the practical problems of religion as a method of life. Religion had been to me, and those about me, far too concrete a thing for that to happen. The book on mysticism once completed, the time seemed to have come for me to turn to the problem of the reconstruction of our religious practices so as to harmonize them with modern knowledge. *God or Man? A Study of the Value of God to Man* was the result of that effort. In this title, "God" means again the God of the religions as they exist among us, i.e., a superhuman being with whom social relations can be maintained.

The main problem of *God or Man?* is formulated thus in the Preface: " 'What God exists?' is a question about which I have had very little to say here, for I have tried to remain within the range of human knowledge . . . the more important, or, in any case, the more urgent and profitable task before humanity to-day is not to obtain a reliable definition of God, but to learn how, by what method or technique, what is accounted good—and by some called 'divine' —can be secured by man or incarnated in human nature." The problem may be stated somewhat differently, and more pointedly thus: Are the fruits of traditional religion really due to the intervention of the God worshipped, or does the religious method set in activity forces resident in human nature, of which science is slowly gaining the mastery, and which it is learning to use far more effectively than they have ever been used in religious worship? Are there, in short, two kinds of available forces, one divine and the other human; the first called upon in the worship of God and the second in secular activity?

The central part of the volume is accordingly a study of the fruitfulness of religious worship, with the purpose of discovering the forces actually involved in cures of body and mind, moral improvement, joy, peace, etc., when these blessings follow upon worship. It appears clearly that in the alleged actions of God in man, natural, known forces are present, and that these forces are adequate to produce the effects attributed to God. Thus, one is led to the conclusion that the present task of humanity is to learn to use these physiological and psychical forces in the best, the most effective way, without letting itself be retarded by the persistency of an obsolete method—the only thinkable one two thousand years ago.

"As a matter of fact, the religious method is already superseded almost completely in the physical and the physiological realms. In so far as most educated Christians are concerned, the physical universe has been turned over to the engineer, disease to the physician, and intellectual education to the lay teacher; and, instead of being accounted a loss, the change is regarded by most Christians as of incalculable value.

"In the moral realm also, the religious method is rapidly being displaced. In the hands of specialists in character formation and reformation, scientific methods prove their superiority and crowd the religions out of a sphere of activity which they have long regarded as pre-eminently their own" (p. 299).

"The systematic introduction of scientific management for the establishment of accepted individual and social ideals in the mind of the young for purging the individual from evil tendencies, and for the organization of the life impulses into harmonious personalities will mark a new era in the history of humanity."

The last chapter of *God or Man?* includes a section on new churches and their functions. The disappearance of the method of the traditional churches will not involve the loss of any genuine source of power. On the contrary, it will mark the passage from a less to a more effective way of using the forces that are at the service of man.

Many years have passed since my search for knowledge about the nature of religion and its value to humanity began. Am I satisfied with the practical outcome of it? Occasionally I meet people who deplore the influence of my writings. I do not refer to the worldly wise in enjoyment of wealth and influence who want to preserve at all cost, for the masses, a religion preaching humility, obedience to established authority, and renouncement of earthly possessions in exchange for the imperishable treasures of heaven. Those to whom I refer are less disingenuous persons who ask, "Are you yourself a bit happier for your negations?" I have long ago faced that question, and I am free to confess that the existence of a Good Shepherd, a perfect, all-powerful Friend, would, at times, be a most comfortable and encouraging thought; and also that an uncritical belief in continuation after death would lull to sleep occasional painful yearnings. But, is one free to believe what one would like to believe, and is disregard or ignorance of the truth necessary to a happy and worthwhile life? The problem is a complex one. If, in some ways, faith in a social god and immortality works for good, in other ways it does harm—a harm to which the faithful are blind. They establish the budget of religion as if there was no debit. What the grave evils inherent in the two cardinal beliefs of the Christian religion are I have tried to say in two chapters of *God or Man?*

If I look with an easy conscience upon whatever incidental unfortunate results my writings may have, it is because I am persuaded that the harm done by our traditional religion to populations at the present highest level of knowledge and social training, is no longer to be ignored, and because of the conviction that the religious method can be replaced with great profit to civilized humanity; the necessary knowledge for that replacement is at hand. Methods, far better than the worship of gods, not only for the control of physical nature, but for the enhancement of the spiritual life, are now available.

It is only if the insufficiency of an antiquated social structure is felt, and if a passionate wave of belief in the possibility of a better order is aroused that humanity may be expected to turn with an irresistible determination to the reconstruction of bankrupt institutions built in times of ignorance.

There is among us a large number of well-intentioned persons of influence who go to great length to hide their disbelief. The masses, they think, are not able to live decently without the support provided by the religion they profess, and a too sudden and widespread loss of belief would threaten the very foundation of society. The truth seems to be, rather, that by placing their influence on the wrong side of the scale, these people prevent moral progress at a normal and safe rate. Progress results from a conflict of opinions. To suppress one's opinion is to pervert the natural course of development. One may safely take it that, human nature being what it is, the resistance offered by the ignorance and the temper which make a Fundamentalist will be a sufficient break upon too hasty changes in religion.

My philosophy is simple, it does not penetrate far into the metaphysical realm. Stupidity and cruelty, as well as intelligence and goodness, seem manifested in the universe. How to reconcile these opposites, I do not know. The systems of philosophy with which I am acquainted leave me quite unconvinced.

There is, however, one fact of enormous significance, a fact incontestable and verifiable by everyone: an urge works in man—it is present already in the animal world—to create the perfect in every aspect of life. For the perfect in art, science, and conduct, some men will sacrifice their lives; and all will admire the sacrifice. How does that fact bear upon the problem of God and Immortality? To that query I can give only halting and incomplete answers. But I know that, apart from all reasoning, there is satisfaction in beauty, truth, and affection. A life of devotion to the ideal is good, now and in itself. The high delight procured by such a life does not depend upon the existence of a God or the eternity of man; it is good in itself. That is sufficient to give dignity and worth to life.

Am I satisfied with this limited assurance? Very far from it. The renunciation of knowledge is painful and, under certain circumstances, tragic indeed. It is precisely in order to relieve that tragedy that the heavenly Good Shepherd has been invented. But if the comforting dream has to be given up we have acquired in exchange more efficacious means for realizing, in part at least, the end described by the Christian religion as the "Kingdom of God upon earth." To draw attention to those means has been my chief concern in *God or Man?*

BIBLIOGRAPHY

Studies in the Psychology of Religious Phenomena—Conversion, *American Journal of Psychology*, vol. vii, 1896.

Les Tendances fondamentales des mystiques chrétiens, *Revue philosophique*. Paris. 1902. Pp. 1–36, 441–87.

A Psychological Study of Religion. Macmillan & Co., New York. 1912.

The Belief in God and Immortality. New York. 1916.
  Second Edition. Chicago, Open Court Publishing Co.

The Psychology of Religious Mysticism. London: Kegan Paul, Trench, Trübner & Co; and New York: Harcourt & Brace. 1925.

God or Man? A Study of the Value of God to Man. New York: Henry Holt & Co. 1934.

The Reconstruction of the Churches.

Religion's Use of Me

by

EDWIN D. STARBUCK

*Director of Character Research, Professor of Philosophy and Psychology,
The University of Southern California*

WHEN one sets about the task of thinking, it is well
to do a bit of self-criticism, for the mind must of
necessity interpret the world through the media of
its own images, probably quite coloured, distorted,
and selected. There is need of even greater caution
when one undertakes to discuss the object of one's
emotional life, for the feelings capture the thoughts
and make them their servants. Most difficult of all is
right thinking about religion for it is in this sphere
probably that one best catches the *whole* person in
the act of thinking and feeling most *vitally*, and therefore most selectively.

The task is not hopeless, for a student of religion
being also a psychologist, has met constantly the
chronic tendency of the mind to project its own
states all around the landscape and has thus learned
some caution. He knows quite well that his most
meticulous "scientific" conclusions may be the
rationalization of his temper and passions. He learns
that to develop a critique of himself is his first duty,
to correct his eccentricities his second, and to report
with discrimination and moderation the third and last.

From much of the difficulty under discussion there

is no escape. The mind cannot free itself from its blindnesses and prejudices any more than a body can cast off its own skin. The mind, however, does become sufficiently agile to play fact against fact, evidence against evidence, doubt against doubt, and theory against theory until it gains some disciplined insight. It is a distinctive mark of the psychology of religion that students with all their differences in temperament and training have had such high intellectual fellowship and so few severe antagonisms.

In the case of this individual who, incited by an eager editor, must now become the specimen for observation in the Psychology of Religion Museum, there is much to be accounted for and yet more to be explained away. Since it is a psychological museum and is not open to ready observation, a few frank confessions are the only way rightly to reveal the twists and strains, the passions and eccentricities that colour and distort whatever achievement there has been.

In the first place it is hardly correct to say that I have worked at the Psychology of Religion. The greater truth is the other way about. It has worked at me. Since adolescence there has been an irresistible urge—a driving force acting sometimes outside of the personality, sometimes as a part of the very selfhood, impelling in that direction. My "mission"—it has always felt like a sort of "calling"—has been to try to render thinkable and usable the illusive reals of religion. This obsession has shifted along the years through many phases: zeal for understanding, teach-

ing, and expounding the Old and New Testament—
a zeal that found an outlet as a teacher of Sunday
school; missionary enthusiasms; the application of
scientific concepts to the wonder tales and miracles;
historical and sociological orientation; philosophical
revaluation; psychological analysis and synthesis
based upon an immediate study of the facts of personal
experience. Regardless of the particular outlet for
expression, the obsession is always present and gains
momentum through the years.

In the second place the subject of this sketch has
been afflicted with a sort of chronic religiosity. How
can he therefore be a true student when he is a partial
pleader? During the middle years of college life
when doubts were fiercest and the casting of outworn
beliefs into the dump heap of superstition was most
in evidence, there was "as from a subterranean depth
upborne" a constructive attitude towards religion
which made it possible to work throughout the
college years sympathetically and happily with the
Christian associations and with the United Presbyterians, as teacher and choir leader. In spite of all
inner rebellions and outer impatience that constructive attitude was moving on. A most valued schoolmate
remarked to a group of his friends, who were also my
friends, "Oh, yes, Starbuck is all *right*, only he is
dyed-in-the-wool religious." When my first book,
The Psychology of Religion, appeared, Elbert Hubbard
reviewed it in *The Philistine* and dubbed the author
an "attorney of the church trust." Boris Sidis in his

book *Psychology of Suggestion* remarked that the trouble with the author is that he doesn't seem to know that conversion is a pathological phenomenon. The advocate brought before the court of justice!

More damaging still, there is a persistent ineradicable mysticism in this would-be student of religion. Perhaps he discovers only what he himself feels and might save himself the bother. There has always been a kind of all-overishness and all-throughishness in whatever he has been occupied with whether it be "work, play, love, or worship." Not infrequently has this mystical quality been pointed out by his friends and critics. Dr. Rachel Knight dedicated her book *The Founder of Quakerism* to the teacher under whose direction it was done, calling him "Scientist, philosopher, Quaker, mystic. . . ." Dr. George A. Coe wrote an illuminating article entitled "Modern Mystics," in which he properly impaled James, Starbuck, and others as the outstanding examples. Starbuck's chief offence was an article entitled "The Feelings and Their Place in Religion." This has been the object of incisive criticism. To such charges there has never been a word of reply, for to a certain degree they are justified. While criticisms are in order, they are not adequate. This student has entertained always an ugly prejudice against all radical mysticisms and a craving for intellectual understanding.

Along with the mystical immediacy of the religious experience and its "mighty inwardness," there has run through the years a philosophy or theology to

match. It might be described as a sort of pantheism—
or panpsychism or pankalonism—a sense of an Inter-
fusing Presence. Creator gods and absentee deities
have never seemed to possess any potency. In childhood there were floating images: a flaming sword,
tablets of stone, parting of waters, healing of diseases.
These pictures, however, seemed evanescent and
fanciful, while the feeling of a Presence has had body
and substance. Yes, it would seem that the dice are
loaded. The wealth from the intellectual conjuring
was already in the till.

These and other items that would be worth recording are only half the story. There probably never has
been a more persistent and stubborn doubter. The
negations have never been altogether, not even
predominantly, destructive, for they have been held
in check by insatiable hungers reaching in every direction, including the wish sufficiently to rationalize
religion as to make much of it thinkable, understand-
able, and controllable.

Throughout high-school and college life subjects
were chosen from the most diverse fields: seven years
of mathematics; one year of astronomy; six years
of Latin; laboratory courses in biology, embryology,
physics, chemistry; a good many semesters in history,
literature, psychology; also geology, French, German,
and several other subjects. Never a dull course. All
of them were absorbingly interesting. The achievement was sufficiently satisfactory to win scholastic
honours and to bring unsolicited positions as teacher

in Latin and mathematics, both of which lay outside the field of the major interest, and later, in education and psychology. In the study of religion there has been a similar omnivorous appetite and catholicity of sympathy. Not one of the great religions and hardly one of the minor cults has failed to furnish some sort of sustenance to the spiritual life.

This warring between tenderness and toughness, between acceptance and doubt, between inner sensitivity and vigorous intellectuality are only samples from among a number of conflicting eccentricities: dynamic, heavily muscled for work and play, at the same time with irresistible cultural urges and a well-developed inner sanctuary of worth and meaning: an imagination intrigued with plots, plans, and programmes—many of them extending into the long future—and at the same time a dullness of fancy that must stubbornly wrestle with a "problem" almost endlessly before it reaches clarification; devotion to both art and the sciences; strong sensory appeal and keen recognition of ideal values; optimism and pessimism; timidity that can hardly face an audience with equanimity, then, when the inhibitions are off, the voice of an enthusiast and would-be prophet. What a menagerie! Some of the beasts in this collection have many a jolly tussle. Others have long-drawn conflicts.

There have been, strangely, certain areas of mentality for which there are no adequate compensations and which must, therefore, stand as simple human weaknesses: over-conscientious; sensitive; chronically sympathetic; ridiculously suggestible even to the point of gullibility; shockingly indifferent to wealth and name and fame; no fear of death; no concern about personal continuance; no felt need of the conserving presence of some Absolute. There is an inner confidence in Life, in Truth, in Beauty, that cuts under these passions that excite most men, and renders them just curious rather than crucial.

It has seemed certain that the heritage and up-bringing of the subject of this sketch directly accounts for nearly everything that has happened—tastes, attitudes, aptitudes, temperamental eccentricities, religious peculiarities. The mental and spiritual weathers in which he was immersed were intense, pervasive, impelling, and inviting.

BIRTH AND UPBRINGING

The home was in the country a dozen miles south-west of Indianapolis. Woodlands interspersed with fertile fields stretched away seemingly without end. The house was an ample and well-appointed one for those years. Along with a smokehouse and a springhouse it was of brick, made with clay tramped out under the feet of oxen. It stands in perfect condition after nearly a century. It was placed near a perpetual clear spring that was the stopping-and-chatting-place for neighbours for many miles around. In four directions at distances of from three to four miles were villages that were places to linger for small-talk after the errands were done. Our community, being only a few miles from everywhere, was called Centre Neighbourhood. Having no Post Office, its interests focused around the school and the "meeting-house." It was here at the church that the neighbours gathered on First Day morning and for prayer-meeting Sabbath evening. Most of them dropped their work on Fourth Day morning at eleven o'clock for their mid-week meeting. In all the five communities nearly everybody knew and liked everyone. Beyond these were other neighbourhoods that seemed to extend on and on. They were friendly Quaker communities. Not a case of serious bickering—certainly not a feud or lawsuit—can I recall.

There was much visiting and banqueting, especially on First Day after meeting. There were happy, informal games on that day, but no organized sports, or croquet, or swimming, for these would desecrate the sacredness of the day. On weekdays there were sports of many kinds. Evenings might bring sociables with charades and old-fashioned games. Authors but never cards. The Virginia Reel and other simple steps to the music of the "fiddle" but no *dancing*, which was sinful. There were corn-huskings, log-rollings, barn-raisings, and many other festive occasions. If there was illness the neighbours vied with one another for the privilege of taking the nightly shifts in sitting up with the sick.

Those simple-minded Quaker folk didn't talk much about religion; they took it for granted. Nor did they profess religion in those earlier years before the infusion of Methodism with its experience meetings; they *lived* it. Often the best meetings were those in which not a word was spoken. All were "waiting on the Lord" and feeling the common satisfactions of the indwelling presence of the Spirit. Each was supposed to remain silent unless the Holy Spirit gave him utterance. He should be guided by the "Light that lighteth everyone who cometh into the world." There were also the daily devotions following breakfast, with Bible readings and a few spoken words, or none, until it should seem time to melt away into the work of the day.

Participating vocally in a primitive Quaker meeting was often a matter of a struggle and a battle. I sometimes watched the play of emotions on the countenance of my father, who usually sat as head of the meeting, next to the partition which separated the men and women, on the "facing-bench," among the elders, and in full view of the rest of us. Sometimes his face would colour a deep red. Really being a gentle, modest man he would have much preferred that the Spirit would let him alone. In spite of himself the lips would begin to move, the body to show signs of restlessness, and not infrequently did the Spirit win against the reluctant flesh. In the case of mother, a bashful, retiring soul, the Spirit usually lost out. I knew myself the awfulness of that struggle. Having as a youth borne testimony a couple of times in a fairly acceptable manner, I was prompted towards faithfulness in that direction by Candace Mills, Lizzie Pruett, and other loving friends. But *could* I! Sometimes in looking ahead to a forthcoming meeting I experienced a luscious pain, mingled with nine parts dread, that was hard to bear. I learned through tough experience that there was no right way out of it except the path that led straight through to victory. That unspoken eloquence of the Quakers was something for which there are no fitting words of description. I recall one day going back in the two-seated carriage from the Newbys', where we had been visiting. I was seated with mother on the back seat, with father and a next older brother in front. Mother noticed in my hand a smooth, ellipsoidal, water-worn stone. She wished to know where I found it. I confessed almost in a whisper that I had brought it from among the playthings of the Newby boys. Not a word was spoken, then, or after, or ever. But when father reached the next crossroad he turned the horses back and drove the mile and a half. The young culprit certainly felt like a criminal going to his doom. Without a word of command the stone was returned, and silently, except for the usual conversation, the journey home was resumed. A hundred sermons on respect for property never could have sunk so deep.

Conscientiousness? Duty? Helpfulness? Such words were probably never used. They were not needful, for the ideas they are supposed to symbolize were swallowed up in the fact of entering cheerfully into the common life. There were endless chores. Plenty of drudgery. So many animals to feed. It was a pleasure to gratify their excellent appetites. So many cows to be milked. So many horses to be fed and curried. All the cows and horses were personalities and had names. We talked and laughed about their eccentricities. So many miles of corn-rows to be traversed and so many acres of grain to be reaped. We vied with each other zestfully in what otherwise would have been slavish work. Scarcely a harsh word among those seven boys and their two sisters. Plenty of raillery and a bit of witty sarcasm too often directed, I thought, at the much spoiled youngest, who was in danger of cultivating vanities. Almost no punishments. About the severest word of the father when some fairly unseemly act was done was "fie! fie!" or "tut! tut!" We used invariably the plain language, *thee* and *thou*. It would have seemed sacrilege to have addressed our parents or any older person in so-called polite speech. About the worst profanity we children ever uttered was to speak to a brother or a sister with a *you* instead of a *thee*. No, the moral laws were usually not "observed," they were written on the heart.

People in those communities, including the Starbuck family, were healthy-minded, healthy-bodied creatures. By extraction New Englanders and North European. Our forebears were Nordics out of England. The earliest Starbucks in America were whale-fishers off Nantucket Island. Later they wandered, and pressed their way through the wilderness into Carolina and on into Ohio and Indiana. They were always overdue, a restless lot mentally and physically. The seven brothers and two sisters scattered as far as the nation was long and into many vocations. The next generation, our own children, six of them, likewise by their own choosing have spread the length of the land and into as many vocational interests as their number allows. All are zestful mentally, watching too much the far horizons. The oldest son entered the war as an aviator and was written up in one of the magazines, along with his father, under the caption "Pioneer, New Style." It is in the breed and the blood, in the tradition.

HIGH-SCHOOL DAYS (1881–4)

In those years academies were scattered all about the Middle West, Quaker academies among them. I first attended one of these near home. The last two years were spent some distance away on account of the principalship of Absalom Rosenberger, an Earlham College mate of my older brothers and sister. He was a person of rare quality and afterwards became President of Penn College and later of Whittier College. He had gathered around him a fine coterie of teachers. Among them were Clint Sherrick, who smiled and chuckled through algebra and geometry, intriguing us into the belief that they were really exciting, and Ira Cammack, who was later for so many years the distinguished superintendent of the Kansas City schools. These were rich though uneventful years, with the usual adolescent foolishness, chums, sociability, intra-mural, and inter-academic athletics, artistic effusions stimulated by literary societies, and the usual absorption in studies that were made inviting. Religiously, the atmosphere was entirely free. It was gentle, sincere, and distinctly non-evangelistic. There was a note of personal responsibility that contained something of a universal note. Being one of the student Commencement speakers, I delivered an oration which sounded a clarion call to America to preserve the Puritan traditions. It was so full and round that it was beyond the expectancy of teachers and fond relatives alike, not to say a good deal of a surprise to the orator himself.

FIRST TEACHING (1884–6)

The expectancies ran in the direction of going to college. It was necessary to earn the means for paying the expense of it. If one lived at home $40.00 a month seemed more than sufficient. Teaching would provide that munificent sum. The most natural thing was to turn to teaching. The natural place to begin was in a nearby neighbourhood where there was a vacancy, and then in the home school. That vocation had been made glorious through the fine personalities of Mary Wright, Jennie Wright, Emma Mills, and other teachers who had brought the spirit of Earlham and other colleges into those neighbourhoods. Those two were years of genuine ripening and integration. It was necessary to be more than a whole person to meet the standards which had been set and the expectancies of relatives and neighbours. I threw into it every ounce I had. Sometimes, coming home from the long day of eight until four, plus the long hours of early morning preparation for the classes, I would lie down for a little rest and fall into so deep a sleep that it was necessary for the family to coax the mind back to consciousness through the use of cold cloths and tender hands across the face. A new schoolhouse had been built in the home neighbourhood. It was a picnic to beautify the grounds and to make the appointments right within and without. No. 1 schoolhouse still stands. After the movement toward consolidation made the building superfluous it was converted into a storehouse for a farmer's machinery. There still smile down at the mowers and reapers of this machine age the three great attractively lettered words, Accuracy, Faithfulness, Righteousness, occupying the main space above the blackboard and standing as symbols of the spirit that tried to actuate those happy, busy days of school life.

The teacher was expected to stand as the live spiritual nerve of the community outside as well as within the school. That was no strain, for it was in tune with a feeling of life's values. An event that needs recording, which was not a real event except outwardly, was a public acceptance of Christianity during that second year of teaching. Revivalism and Evangelism were sweeping those serene Quaker communities. Cutting sharply across the spirit of Quakerism was the notion that one must have a definite conversion experience. In the heat of the revival at Centre meetings I went through the forms of this public acceptance, not feeling at the moment the negative implication that my heart had not been on the whole "given to the Lord" during the preceding months. It gave the revivalists the pleasure of counting one more recruit, and it gave the devotee the satisfaction of trying to play the game with earnest people. An older brother, Elwood, who had no particular "sins" that needed renouncing, fell for the same stunts, then went into seclusion for days afterward, feeling that he had quite made a fool of himself.

Doubts were naturally deepening—the authority of the Old Testament, the miracles, the birth stories, the mission of Jesus, and all the rest of it. The dramatic battle was on between Adam and the monkey. Earlham College not so far away was distinctly on the side of evolutionism, though it was presented to the innocent public in homeopathic doses sugared over with a very genuine religiosity. The flames were much stirred up by the freethinkers who taught and spoke. David Starr Jordan, with his radical notions, had been a teacher in an Indianapolis high school and on occasion gave an unequivocal lecture. He was now president of

Indiana University forty miles away. The discussions of evolution added zest to the collegiate passions. The way to Earlham College was already paved by two brothers and a sister, but the path was broken also toward Indiana University by my oldest brother. To the university I would go. To the very storm-centre of the new thinking! I would find the facts and take up the fight.

Everything was elective in those revolutionary college days under the young Jordan. I immediately swung into geology with him and into descriptive and experimental biology with Kingsley, a simon-pure geneticist. Evolutionism was winning. What a long-drawn, hard battle. Old moorings giving way. Tempestuous seas ahead. Old friendships threatened. Already the words *atheist* and *infidel* were trembling and throbbing on the lips of my old neighbours back home. The challenge of being faithful to "the truth" gave courage but not peace. The struggles were carried often into long hours of wakeful nights. Sometimes a bit of a tear. No praying. It must be fought out in the arena of straight thinking. There was no revolution but a terribly profound reconstruction. There was some truth in the Bible despite the myth and the childlike philosophy. It was mine to help find it. The life-line to which I clung was that word Truth, a rationalization for the convenience of a troubled soul. I was able to formulate for myself the new world of values in about these words: "You have been trying to *make* truth out of your own small thinking.

It is better and nobler to *find* truth, accept it, and take the consequences."

The world view which was developing as a result of many electives in the physical sciences and with history under Dabney, who was much influenced by Buckle and all those who knew that man was but a creature of terrestrial forces, was that of an earth-hugging naturalism and a pretty complete functionalism. But the humanitarian interests never weakened. They flowed through the channels of a new Humanism. There was the constant temptation to go forth with a flaming sword and destroy superstitions. That impulse was held in check by a genuine affection for neighbours, friends, and acquaintances and a determination never to wound their religious sensibilities, but to work constructively for the things we held in common. For the most part I was able to do so and without ever falsifying that precious word *truth*, or playing the part of a hypocrite. I even worked sympathetically and constructively during the last three years of college life with the fine and devout United Presbyterians. Although, out of fairness to their traditions, it was necessary for me to withdraw—against their protest—from teaching Sunday-school classes, it was possible to lead the choir during the last three years and enter into most of the activities of the church.

There were two indications of the constructive way in which the new vision was working in the free atmosphere of that university. A number of students of like mind formed an intimate group for weekly study and discussion that passed under the mystic symbol B H C. Among its members were Edward Howard Griggs, Sam Harding, Russel Ratliff, Carolyn Brown, and a dozen others. Had the deep, dark secret of those three letters been told to the world they would have spelled out—B-r-o-w-n-i-n-g H-e-r-e-t-i-c C-l-u-b. We studied Browning intensively. That poet, whom we admired, was only the point of departure for exploring and synthesizing the various fields of culture. The soul of the New Humanism was taking shape in us. The other event indicative of the quiet revolution that was going on was the change in temper and the reconstruction of the constitution of the Y.M.C.A., a society which held a significant place in the university. That association had been too Bible-centred and evangelical, too partisan and sectarian for the new age. Tatlock, Miss Fisher, Mark K. Polk, Starbuck, and others thought that they should disband definitely and officially the local Y.M.C.A. and establish the Indiana University Religious Association, open to any and all, of every faith and no faith, whose lives were committed to the search for ideals and the welfare of humanity. The movement won out and was a power in the place. Only after the prime movers had all graduated and gone away from the university, and the Y.M.C.A. had become more modern and cosmopolitan in its attitudes, was its central organization able to restore the affiliation that had been set aside.

The philosophy or religion of Humanism was soon transcended. I had already chosen philosophy as a major. Under the stimulating tutelage of William Lowe Bryan and other teachers there was developing a religion of philosophy and a philosophy of religion. I was wrestling with scholars—Plato, Aristotle, Plotinus, Leibnitz, Hegel—whose world view was so ample that they didn't seem to know the difference between philosophy and religion. The appreciation of religion for whatever worth it had was already a persistent way of thinking. The philosophers were putting into Humanism body and substance, organization and perspective, universality and meaning. I fell hard for Aristotle's dynamic interpretation of reality. I became a grateful devotee of the monadology of Leibnitz. So with Spinoza. Berkeley seemed irrefutable and irresistible. Most drawing of all was Hegel. In fact, when it happened that I must be one of the six Commencement orators, the topic chosen was "The Unity of Opposites." Out of strife and conflict, the higher harmony. Many of the audience seemed moved by the appeal so enthusiastically presented by this young prophet of the new order. My indulgent professor of philosophy penned this inscription on a programme and sent it to the platform: "Oh Life! Oh beautiful rainbow! With all the rays leading out into the infinite white." This philosophical illumination carried over into the postgraduate Harvard years.

A flash that cleared the skies and precipitated afresh

the sense of the Universal Soul of religion was the appearance just at that time of James Freeman Clarke's *Ten Great Religions*. That work was devoured eagerly. It was food and drink. Religion is universally human. The interest spread. During my senior year I found myself directing a Sunday afternoon study group of more than half a hundred. We used Clarke's books as a point of departure for lively discussions.

AN INTERIM OF TEACHING AND GROWTH (1890–3)

All the lines were leading inevitably in the direction of a career in the study of philosophy with special emphasis on religion. College life had been accomplished through self-support. At graduation it seemed wise to enhance the modest resources. Spiceland (Indiana) Academy was seeking a teacher of Latin and mathematics. An invitation to take that position came as a happy surprise. A year later there came the offer of the professorship in mathematics at Vincennes University. The teaching there covered the usual subjects, including advanced algebra, calculus, surveying, and astronomy. Here was the opportunity to teach an exact science as an art. This ideal was but the fruitage of the influence of Rufus Green and Joseph Swain at Indiana University. We, their students, often remarked that they were artists. Like the notes to music was their handling of the techniques of the subject. Always the mystic, I was deeply moved by this approach and was impelled to share the inspiration with my own students.

During those busy years there was much reading on the side in the great literatures of religion and philosophy. The persistent passion to be an interpreter of the profounder values was shocked into fresh life, repolarized and crystallized during the first year at Vincennes by Max Müller's book, *Lectures on the Science of Religion*, which had just come into my hands. There, before one's eyes philology and history were presenting the long story of the development of the cultures of India and showing their bearing on the thought of the Occident. There was thrown into the crucible the psychological passions that had been developing during college life. I read a paper before the Indiana State Teachers' Association at Indianapolis during the Christmas holidays of 1892 on the science of religion and its place in education. Stress was put on the psychological groundwork of such a study. That was about as clear an outline of this new science and its possibilities as I have been able to formulate up to the present time. There could be no delay. Catalogues of all the leading universities were studied. So slight an offering appeared. One leading university listed a course in the history of religion and announced that the object of the course was to show that the Christian religion was the only one capable of rational justification. Harvard almost alone offered courses that seemed dispassionate and that promised assistance—one by C. C. Everett and one by Francis G. Peabody. Furthermore, Harvard had a great constellation of outstanding men in philosophy and psychology.

HARVARD YEARS (1893-5)

Stimulating years. Seasoned scholars. An atmosphere of serious study. A vigorous Philosophy Club of staff and students and a small select Philosophical Club for intimate discussions. Lecture courses given with dignity and high spirit.

Knowing that foundations for techniques and methods for the study of religion must be laid, two courses in psychology, one descriptive and the other experimental, were taken with Münsterberg, and one with William James. The most enthusiastic proclaimers of scientific method, for which my soul was crying out, were the historians. Consequently a course and a seminar were chosen with Emerton. The "science" involved was twofold: respect for fact versus theory; and the use of careful, discriminating thinking, always challenged by the facts.

The obstacle in the way of attacking the psychology of religion with undivided application was that in those early days at Harvard no credit could be obtained for work that was not done in courses. However, the work could be and was done on the side with persistency and unabated enthusiasm. How could it proceed? The central guiding principle was that the study must deal *primarily with the first-hand religious experience of individuals*, not so much with their *theories* about religion as with their actual *experiences*. One's thoughts concerning religion are once removed from the vital springs of conduct and valuation. Sociological theories, historical records, and philosophical doctrines are thrice removed, and consist for aught we know of only congealed, discoloured, and distorted semblances of real experience. One must catch at first hand the feelings of spirituality. I would institute a sort of scholastic confessional. I assembled sets of incisive questions, inexcusably innocent of the fact that Galton had already invented and used the device of the questionnaire. I began with my friends and acquaintances as a guarantee of the sincerity of the confession. Would they be willing to record certain significant happenings in their own religious experience or the absence of such experiences? The best success would come from a study of those events that had or were supposed to have specific and sharp definition such as the feelings of divine presence, answer to prayer, actual feelings of the sense of communion during the ceremony of communion, and the like. Perhaps the most dramatic single storm-centre of religious experience was to be found in conversion. I would begin with that and move in as many directions as possible.

Late in 1893 I formulated and began to circulate one questionnaire on conversion, another on the breaking of habits, a third and more elaborate one, four pages in length, on the lines of religious development not attended by conversion. Reproductions of the first and third of these are presented herewith.

Strangely, the venture did meet with pretty general acceptance. An acquaintance, approached either personally or by letter, rarely failed to respond. A few teachers were intrigued with the idea and through them I was able to secure small total populations. To my surprise even churches were receptive to the idea and proved to be constructively helpful.

It was a source of profound gratitude to the respondents that the answers were so painstaking and so manifestly sincere. This thoroughness and evident sincerity were noted by James in his introduction to my book, *The Psychology of Religion*, after he had looked through several hundred of the documents which it had been my pleasure to lend him while he was preparing the Gifford Lectures.

Faculty members received the notion of such a study with moods varying from encouragement to vexation, mostly the former. Everett looked over the first draft of the sheet on conversion, smiled and wished it success. On the other hand, James examined it more than cursorily and offered valuable suggestions. Later he volunteered to sign the document and to indicate that it was being circulated with his approval. In the interest of his good name I stoutly protested. His insistence overrode the argument. Great was my astonishment when he presented me at the next meeting of the class with a copy of the question sheet bearing his own signature along with that of C. C. Everett,

If you have ever experienced Conversion, whether instantaneous or otherwise, will you write your experience as minutely as possible for the following points about it:

1) Symptoms and motives which preceded and accompanied it.

2) Circumstances of your life at the time of Conversion.

3) Comparison of life before and after.

4) What part of the Conversion was unusual light, change in feelings, motives & conception of detail; change in understanding or unusualness?

5) Describe any unusual sights, sounds, or events at the time.

6) Any relapse from the first experience; Can we understand it up in similar way; & if any, age; never sued it draw away.

If you have experienced it, please write up it in similar way it drew never away.

Think your conversion sudden, notmade it, its development, unusual light, change in feelings. If any experience, a large & varied experience (if any). Their experience is very valuable to us to reach conclusions concerning the study of the spiritual life.

Return answers to:
Edwin D. Starbuck
11 Rowland St
Cambridge, Mass.

Recommended undertaken in the name of:
C. C. Everett, Dean Howard Divinity School
William James, Prof. of Psychology, Harvard.
Rev. Alexander McKenzie, of Cambridge

1. What does religion mean to you? Does it necessarily involve certain (a) feelings or emotions, (b) intellectual notions or definite beliefs, (c) action or conduct? and specify what in each case.

Religion means to me a feeling of love and
worship for a Supreme Power which is all good-
It involves (a) a sense of mystery- and a desire to
be like or as nearly like it I can to the Power
(b) an idea or notion that there must be something
besides natural laws to control the Universe- I mean
something that instituted those laws-

(c)- My conduct is
more like the
to me-

2. Does it seem to you that so

Some kind of re
necessary

3. What would it mean to yo
church? What is that without which

b) My feelings would
then I would feel
fits of this Blue-
Bible- and I think
charity is that it is
people-

Alameda, Cal-
Dec. 6. 1894-

Mr. Edwin E. Starbuck
Dear Sir.
    Professor Earl Barnes
of Leland Stanford Jr. University sent me the enclosed
Circular to fill out.
    I would like to have
answered the questions
more definitely - but they
are rather hard to answer
without saying a great deal-
    He also sent me some
work to be done in my
schoolroom - but I am sorry
to say that I shall not be
able to do it
    If there is anything else

Dean of Harvard's Divinity School, and the revered Dr. McKenzie of the Congregational church near by.

Münsterberg was immoderately impatient. On my particular problem in the laboratory, which was that of how the *ideas* of motion pass over into microscopic bodily movement and somatic changes, he was always meticulously helpful. When it came to seeking some suggestions about the study of religion he was antagonistic and finally explosive. He declared that his problems were those of psychology, while mine belonged to theology, and that they had absolutely nothing to do with each other.

There were picturesque little explosions all over the cultural landscape. Thomas Wentworth Higginson, on seeing the questionnaire on conversion, wrote to James warning him of what seemed certainly a forgery. If such were not the case he wished to register a vigorous protest against this "moral and spiritual vivisection." Dr. Barton, professor of philosophy at Smith College, volunteered to secure confessions from the students in one of his classes, of which the daughter of the Rev. Dr. Smyth was a member. Whereupon her father wrote Dr. Barton saying that if his daughter was to be subjected to such a "spiritual inquisition" he would take her forthwith out of the college. In direct contrast, Dr. J. Estlin Carpenter, principal of Manchester College, Oxford, England, who was Chaplain at Harvard during a part of that year, secured a packet of the questionnaires to use among his students and friends in England.

P

During the winter of 1894–5, about the middle of the second year of the study, some clear and significant consistencies began to appear, particularly in the conversion study: the piling up of age-frequencies near pubescence; likenesses of the phenomena of conversion and those attending the breaking of habits; the signs of the dissociation of personality and its recentering, not unlike the split-personality experiences described by James, Prince, and Janet; and so on through a considerable list. Dean Everett was sufficiently interested to request a report before his class in the philosophy of religion made up of about sixty graduate students which included women as well as men, since Radcliffe students were that year for the first time admitted to graduate courses at Harvard. The presentation was simple and factual and unargumentative. The discussion was then thrown open to the class. That occasion was a sort of christening ceremony for the babe newly born into the family of academic subjects. Some quite hot water was poured into the baptismal font. The first douse of it came from Edward Borncamp, who rose, his face white with emotion. His first sentence, fervid with the warmth of deep conviction, was, "It's all a lie!" Laughter broke out there in that dignified classroom. There was also a pouring of friendly waters into the font, and words of commendation for this new babe. Of course, the attempted damnation of the infant by the first speaker was because its swaddling clothes were only the filthy rags of earthly psychology, ill-becoming the sacredness of religion. The charming Dean, high priest on that occasion, had words of encouragement for the father of the child, and for the offspring itself. There in that class sat Anna Diller, profound student, musician-artist. She warmed towards it and took it to her bosom as she was later to take the whole oncoming Starbuck brood.

A METAPHYSICAL ILLUMINATION

For a half-dozen years and more I had accepted Evolutionism in its fullness. The application of it was complete. Absentee gods and transcendental reals, as magical repositories from which to draw explanatory concepts, had been banished never to return. Berkeley, Kant, and Hume had done their work completely. Yet during those years I, who had studied much in the physical sciences and had taught astronomy, kept falling back into something akin to a stubborn Cartesian dualism. The unconscious desire for a complete and satisfactory synthesis was in no sense the result of "spiritual need," for there was cheerful acceptance of the Universe, and anything it should mete out. It was an ache after an intellectual synthesis. The inner demand was aggravated doubtless by Peabody's picturesque "God," Everett's Hegelian "World Spirit," Royce's monistic idealism, and James's naughty jibes at the Absolute. The problem demanded quiet hours of reflection and dragged the seeker out for long, solitary walks in the evening.

Among the more than Berkeleian considerations which were fighting it out and demanding resolution were these: sensation-perceptions are not the raw data of mentality but are later developing specificities of the wisdom of the organism; creative imagination, and not thought, is the Hamlet of the mental drama; concepts are only the patterned forms of the imagination and symbolize rather than represent "objective" reality. The most stubborn concepts, such as the categories, can be viewed truly either as ejects of the mind or as representations of an external order; hence no *necessary dualism*. The Berkeleian principle could therefore apply universally to stones and stars, to thoughts and appreciations.

On one of my strolls on a side street near the observatory the resolution of these focalized considerations came instantaneously. It was like a recoil from disturbing tensions, an uprush of animation, a sunburst of illumination. Had there been an observer near by he would have thought that a man almost beside himself was running loose on that byway. Words burst forth spontaneously: "I see it! I have it!" Translated into sober English those words meant: "I, a mind, a body-mind, am in and of a universe of meaning. The values of art, religion, human relations, and ideal strivings are at one descriptively, with the formalized objects of thought and perception." Similar though less profound experiences had occurred not infrequently when mulling over some problem. I had learned through the study and teaching of mathematics to press scme ugly problem as far as possible toward a solution and then to lay it aside. Often the problem presented itself already resolved, not infrequently in the night or on the occasion of the early morning awakening. This particular greater, explosive insight which came during those minutes and hours with its fresh feeling of at-home-ness in the universe has deepened through the years. This experience is now for the first time recorded and that only in the interest of veracity, as it fights its way against the impulse to preserve the sacred silences. Yes, Starbuck is hardly fit to interpret the facts of religion dispassionately. Perhaps a *visionaire*. Doubtless of James's "tender-minded" variety.

CLARK UNIVERSITY YEARS (1895–7)

The personal and social surroundings at Harvard were altogether delightful. The master's degree had been meted out as a surprise package. A generous fellowship had been voted. The occupation for the coming months and years must be exclusively with the psychology of religion. There was no way by which such work could receive credit and thus be cashed in toward that academic foible, the degree of PH.D.

An occasional guest during the two Harvard years was an old college mate at Indiana University, Frank Drew. He was a graduate student at Clark University. He told of the entire freedom there for independent study. Few lectures and no requirement to attend them. That was alluring. In the spring of '95 a visit of exploration was made to Worcester. President Hall and his colleagues were hospitable to the notion of transferring residence. A fellowship was granted. The change was made. The year at Clark that stretched to a second was happy and profitable. Hall, Sanford, Burnham, Hodge, and Chamberlain were most helpful, each in his own way.

It turned out that my welcome to Clark was as just one more person added to the academic family and not as a student of religion. Hall made vigorous and persistent efforts to draft me off into some other area of interest. That orange I had sucked dry, he said. For my own benefit it would be better to swing over to an entirely different problem. The advice to the newcomer fell on deaf ears. I had come to Clark for the purpose primarily of continuing the study of religion.

Hall yielded to the insistence, though certainly not with equanimity. While he was dissuading me, he was at the same time assembling periodically a half-dozen students (one of whom was John P. Hylan, my room-mate), picturing the possibilities of the application of psychology to religion and saying that the next ten years at Clark University might well be devoted to studies in that field. I could not help recalling certain events of the spring before. Drew had taken back with him a bundle of the questionnaires to be filled out by Clark students. None were returned.

On the occasion of my visit to Worcester that spring I had found that a Clark student had issued without acknowledgement a syllabus which was almost a reproduction of my original one on conversion and was making it the basis of his doctoral dissertation. Hall himself had prepared a revision of the four-page questionnaire, which he was about to issue, but in this case I was able to prevent its publication.

These sentences now being penned would never see the light were I not commandeered by a stern editor to tell the truth, to record the facts of the rise and development of the psychology of religion. There is no escape. History doesn't lie unless those who help create it fail to conserve its veracities. A psychologist, who knows better than do most persons the organismic nature of mental events and the contradictory cross-currents through human personality, is compelled to be particularly circumspect with the recording of the facts. He must stress equally the picturesque passions of men which the innocent would regard as weaknesses and faults and those which are unqualifiedly heroic.

Hall's was a hungry mind for prestiges and priorities. He never ceased to claim precedence in the psychology of religion or to imply it in writing. (See for example page 382 ff. of his *Life and Confessions of a Psychologist*.) This case ran parallel with his already published statement that he, and not James, was the first teacher of experimental psychology in the United States and that the first laboratory in that field in America was at Johns Hopkins, and not at Harvard. There were many such instances. When the leading psychologists had corrected these errors the claimant clearly lost on every count. (See for example Chapter LII of Ralph Barton Perry's *The Thought and Character of William James*.) The items recorded and suggested here were presented in my review of Hall's *Confessions* in the *Journal of Philosophy*, March 13, 1924. That was well within the span of Hall's life, and the facts there recorded were never refuted.

Hall's lack of enthusiasm about my productivity in this field persisted. When my first book, *The Psychology of Religion*, appeared a couple of years later, among the many reviews of it the only unfriendly one in America was in the Journal of which Hall was editor. Constituted as I was such matters were picturesque rather than disturbing.

It should be said mightily and in great sincerity that these items contain no note of real disparagement of Hall. His was probably the most dynamic, passionate and high-strung personality among the psychologists of the world, and at the same time, as is characteristic of genius, fuller of contradiction. Every apparent weakness is only the offside of some greater strength. This sort of thing in all its diversity he has described delightfully in the *Confessions*. It was as impossible in the midst of that surging mentality for him to see the minor things in perspective as for a mighty swollen river to feel out the sources of its many waters and its why and whither. Even the all-wise Jehovah could not well appreciate the pain that lay beyond the point of His glittering sword and so made the appropriation of lands by His "chosen people" an act of righteousness. That is just a way dominant gods and men have. It was the method of "the master of those who know" of Athens and of the sage of Leipzig. Such, in part, is the technique of producing a genius.

Hall's was easily one of the most inspiring minds that it has been my privilege to know. There was never to the last year of his life the slightest restraint in conversing with him. It was always fun to discuss with greatest intensity, and with a note of criticism which he really enjoyed, some of his most pronounced doctrines: mental heredity, sex psychology, and a good many others.

The chief work at Clark was the continuing and perfecting of the questionnaire studies on the basis of a larger assemblage of data. The methods employed, their strengths and weaknesses, and the methods of refinement, are discussed in considerable detail in the introductory chapter to *The Psychology of Religion*. They do not need reiteration here. At the same time foundations were being laid for branching out in several different directions by methods more rigidly scientific. One problem in particular that seemed important for both the psychology of religion and religious education was the spread throughout the organism of a certain idea or activity or experience.

It was called in those days the problem of "formal discipline," and later "transfer of training." It was a crucial problem and is to-day. Do religious ideas carry over into conduct? Do they influence other attitudes toward life? With the help of Anna Diller and the full co-operation of Sanford and Hodge and their two laboratories and several other graduate students, the problem was attacked from four different angles. Would practice in memorizing one kind of material improve one's proficiency in committing to memory other kindred materials?—a problem on which James had worked. The same for arithmetical skills. Thirdly, would correcting an illusion caused by strong prismatic lenses, until the right hand would touch a dot accurately, pass over into a corresponding correction with the left? Fourthly, will stimulation, by the Hodge method of, say, a right cervical ganglion of a decerebrate cat, which depletes the nuclei and the nucleoli in that ganglion, also deplete those of the opposite ganglion and further show its effect forward and backward along the spinal ganglia, as determined by comparing experimental cats with control specimens? The first two types of study gave zero results and so by mistaken judgment were not published. The other two types of research gave clean-cut results, but neither my teachers nor I could interpret them. Perhaps it was the same cerebral centres involved in the correction of the right hand and the behaviour of the left. Perhaps it was a nutritional and other somatic set of functions that caused the apparent spread of fatigue. Again wrongly these results were not published, since we did not appreciate that negative results are often as valuable as positive.

It was expected that I should come up for the Doctor's examination at the end of the first year at Clark. The studies of religion seemed yet too imperfect. Lines of study as groundwork and for equipment were opening in several directions. The degree was granted in the spring of 1897.

STANFORD UNIVERSITY (1897–1903)

Earl Barnes was resigning from the headship of education at Stanford University. I had some acquaintance with him. David Starr Jordan, at that time President of Stanford, remembered my activities at Indiana University and doubtless had looked up the fact that I had worked a good deal in the field of education at Clark University. An offer came to be assistant professor of education at Stanford and to act as head of the department until they could secure someone whose tastes and training were such as to fit him for the permanent headship. The opportunity was particularly congenial since it was specified that I should have liberty to conduct courses in the psychology of religion. There was, at that time, not one chance in a thousand for securing a position as teacher of the psychology of religion. The work in this field was carried on in a seminar for seniors and graduate students that continued with enthusiasm during the six years at Stanford. An array of questionnaires appeared, each on the phase of the psychology of religion representing the interests of the several students. For the first two years the work of the group was focalized pretty sharply around the study of conversion, of adolescent religious phenomena not attended by conversion, and kindred topics. The event that shocked these interests into crystallization was the request of Havelock Ellis that I revise and extend the two main contributions that had been published in the *American Journal of Psychology* and combine them in a volume, which should be a member of *The Contemporary Science Series*. At the end of the two years that consummation was attained. The volume appeared in 1899.

For the next four years a good deal of the work of that seminar was centred on the genetic psychology of the God-idea. The study moved along two lines: first, the securing of samples of God-concepts, using total populations of young people in high school and college; second, the studying of the genetic psychological aspect of the God-experience among cultivated adults. An elaborate questionnaire for grown-ups was issued and sent almost exclusively to persons of high cultural attainment. Almost all those confessions, together with many other valuable papers, were later lost when they were shipped to Richmond, Indiana— an irreparable loss. A good deal of that patient work was picked up and conserved by students later at the

University of Iowa, particularly in a doctor's dissertation of E. L. Mudge, and part of it was published in his volume *The God Experience*. The fruitage of the Stanford years in the study of religion was equal to any reasonable anticipation.

Novelties were introduced in several directions. A three-hour course through the year was ventured by me in educational psychology, probably the first university course in that field. Another course dealt with the genetic aspects of childhood. Doubtless the first course in character education ever offered was introduced in 1898, a two-hour course running through both semesters. A little later a three-hour seminar in the psychology and pedagogy of religion was started.

Most significant and prophetic for the future, outside of the seminar in the psychology of religion, was a course entitled *Applied Physiology and Psycho-Physics*, given by Dr. Snow, professor of hygiene, and myself. A description in the catalogue read: "A presentation of such methods as superintendents, principals and teachers can and should employ in order to gain a somewhat accurate understanding of children's capacities and needs, and consequently, to direct their training intelligently and effectively. Tests will be given for determining the importance of the various sense organs; what each contributes in the individual child in the formation of judgments; the quickness and accuracy of the various mental functions; the variations in any child from the normal type; and the possibility of overcoming certain defects. The work will consist of two hours of lectures with demonstrations, and one period of laboratory work. The laboratory period will be spent in gaining proficiency in the methods of experimentation and in constructing and testing some of the simpler pieces of apparatus."

Such a course, in these days, would be called *Tests and Measurements*. Unlike later devices for testing and measuring which depend largely on pencil-paper procedure, it was based upon experimental devices in the field of psycho-physics. Dr. J. Allen Gilbert had established at Yale, and later at Iowa, quite a number of norms and we were busy determining others. With the help of Newell H. Bullock and half a dozen other graduate students, extensive tests on about twenty mental and physical proficiencies were made on 2,400 schoolchildren in San Jose. That gold-mine of data, partly organized, still exists, and will be put to use as soon as the time to complete it will permit. It was halted temporarily by the taking of a sabbatical year, by the transfer of academic residence to Earlham College in 1904, but most of all by the fact that at that time there burst upon the world the Binet-Simon tests. These tests intrigued the imagination of students everywhere, for they gave the means for applying quick and somewhat helpful, though often distressingly inaccurate, measures to mental ability. Those rapid-fire devices involve imaginary norms which lack concreteness, objectivity and real units of measure. They are comparable to surveying done by pacing, or prescribing eyeglasses without the objective devices of the oculist. There exists now as strongly as in the year 1900 the determination to go far in the direction of *scientific* testing in education—both religious and secular.

The variety of those courses offered at Stanford, viewed externally and with superficial glance, would appear to be diverse and disconnected. Quite the contrary. There was always a central core of interest that had to do with two things: in the first place, the insight into and understanding of the world of values with a mental grip on some laws of their functioning and development; and secondly, the realization in experience of the fruitage of whatever knowledge and wisdom shall be attained. The scientific and the practical have never once been divorced. The lines of thought and activity there begun have continued throughout my academic experience.

A YEAR OF STUDY ABROAD
(1903 – 4)

The most effective and far-reaching line of attack on understanding the subtleties of the moral and religious life seemed to me then to be the uncovering of the mechanisms that lie in behind specific thoughtful behaviours. Entanglement in the James-Lange theory, among other influences, was driving in that direction. Mosso was getting some hold on fatigue and fear through studying the changes that go on in the circulatory system. Experimentation at Copenhagen, Leipzig, Zürich, and Paris was beginning to tap these somatic functions. Anna Diller and I bundled up our little family and went exploring. James advised Paris. Others, of course, suggested Wundt's laboratory. The upshot of it was that we found the liveliest work going on at Meumann's laboratory at the University of Zürich. There we took up residence for the winter. Mrs. Starbuck studied music with Freund and I worked in Meumann's hospitable laboratory, trying to master Mosso's sphygmomanometer and other devices for registering the relationship between bodily changes and the variety of mental processes, and profiting by attendance on lectures and by exchange of work with other students in the laboratory.

EARLHAM COLLEGE (1904-6)

Earlham College had a dream of establishing a school of education. Towards the close of the sabbatical year I was invited to be its director and to try to build it into an entity. The endowments never came and the dream was not realized. Two happy years were spent there among people whose names were household words in our family. They were, however, not fruitful years in the way of research. I had a bit of a laboratory and carried on some of the work started at Stanford and pursued with Meumann. The flames were kept

burning by lecture courses and through contact with
earnest students.

UNIVERSITY OF IOWA (1906–30)

It was a privilege to join the staff of the University of
Iowa as a member of its combined division of philosophy and psychology, and to participate in both
fields. Personal choice guided by those ravenous
hungers led me into teaching first and last about
everything philosophy offers. There was always a
seminar and usually a lecture course in the psychology
of religion. A good many fine studies and doctor's
dissertations were the result.

In 1912 an appeal came from the American Unitarian
Association to help them as consulting psychologist
in the preparation of a course of study in religious
education, which was to revitalize the weakening
churches of their organization. It was just the year
when a sabbatical leave was due from the University
of Iowa and this offer was timely in more senses than
one, for great enthusiasms had developed for saving
humanity through childhood. It was an elaboration
of the Fiske idea in *Meaning of Infancy*, developed
into a passion and a programme quite earth-filling.
I had proclaimed the doctrine to educators and
religionists, calling the topic usually "A Child-Centred
Civilization." Variations of this were: "A Child-
Centred School," "A Child-Centred Church," "World
Peace through Childhood Training," and the like.

Q

The invitation was accepted for the one year and a second year's leave was granted when the hopes were running fairly high. William I. Lawrance, great soul, was director of the American Unitarian Religious Association. Florence Buck, well trained, fine of speech, of real vision, was his assistant. We would build an up-to-date religious education curriculum with thirty texts and manuals. Along with working at the texts with willing workers assisting, we spread the gospel. Within the two years I had addressed more than four hundred groups, usually holding conferences with the officers and workers of various churches. Progress was made, though with great discouragement, the greatest of which was the fact that the American Unitarian Religious Association, quite a going concern, had been sold to the main body of the association for one dollar. They, the A.U.A., could control the funds and did. Traditionalism lay heavy across institutionalized religion, conserving its satisfactions with an *adult-centred Church*. We won, however, in producing some very good manuals, although we were not able to bring the series to completion. It was too nearly a lost cause, a case of the light that failed.

In 1914 I resumed my teaching at Iowa. There was an increasing demand for work in character education as part of the equipment of teachers, and researches came as naturally in that field as they had in the study of religion. Many of the studies lay by their very nature within both fields. An event that hastened the interest in the field of character was the offer by the Character Education Institution of Washington, D.C., of a prize of $20,000 to the Committee that would turn out the best statement of methods in character education. The Committee of Nine, of which I was chairman, won that award in 1921, after two years of very spirited and intense work. It was a complete surprise to every member of the Committee, for we had elected to be true to our convictions instead of following the then predominant custom of indoctrinating children with moral ideas. We believed in a more natural approach in which the integrity of the child's personality was wholly respected, one that consisted in intriguing his imagination, eliciting his active, creative interest, and stirring his impulses by what we chose to call a *dynamic*, or *tactful*, or *sympathetic*, or *creative* method—a method that involved the entire child in his relation to the whole set-up of the school and of society. The victory had deepened our interest, aroused through the activities of those two years of preparing the report, and had the effect also of making the work in character a little more picturesque and attractive to students. Studies were going on at so lively a rate as to attract special attention from the administration of the University. They chose to encourage the work by establishing, as part of the University organization, an Institute of Character Research to be supported by State funds.

In 1925 I was invited to participate as one of the lecturers in that important and permanently endowed foundation, The Institute for the Comparative Study of Human Culture, in Oslo, Norway. Each summer and autumn they invite four or five scholars from all over the world who are able to present to the delegates and general public a series of lectures, each in his chosen field. This conference is under the auspices of the five Scandinavian countries: Norway, Sweden, Denmark, Finland, and Greenland. The stipendiats, or fellows, selected officially by the five Governments, come at the expense of their own countries to listen and confer in seminars. These young men go back as bearers of the thought and spirit of the Institute and become factors in a new international understanding. Such was the intention of the Institute established by the five countries during the World War as a means of doing their part toward what they thought was a more effective way of solving disturbing problems than through war.

My assigned topic was "An Introduction to a Science of Religion." Fourteen laws or principles of scientific procedure were presented as the central thread around which the researches in the psychology of religion up to that time had been organized.

The lectures were well attended. The discussions were lively and resulted in considerable divergence of thought, but nevertheless established many lines of fellowship. One of the centres of thought in that series was a notion, approached both functionally and structurally, that the centre of personality lies in the thalamic regions of the nervous system and the corresponding aspects of mentality. Dr. Monrad-Krohn, superintendent of the State hospital of psychiatry in Oslo, constantly attended the lectures, and presented in the discussion a good deal of first-hand material bearing out this theory. He also extended an invitation to visit the hospital to examine cases which seemed to demonstrate that truth pretty conclusively.

On returning to the United States my first visit was made to three foundations in New York City as a representative of the Institute, bearing the wish that a foundation be established providing American students the opportunity to enjoy that cultural fellowship.

Progressively during those years at the University of Iowa there were turned out many researches, all of them technically sound, scientifically significant, and humanly important. The insistence that the studies should be objective has given them a distinctive quality. To describe them in this connection would be superfluous, for anyone who cares for that knowledge can readily secure it by obtaining the pamphlet, *New Developments in Philosophy*, cited in the bibliography. The studies themselves are available from the University of Iowa Press. These researches lead off in many directions, for it has been my conviction that each student should follow out the problem that means the integration of his own personal thought-life. The university surely exists for the student rather than the student for the university.

Meanwhile European students of religion had been troubled about the radical empiricism of the studies in religion in America. Have the freer-minded scholars of the new world lost their souls in the midst of the rattling techniques? Is it the case, as the *Literatur-Zeitung* had said editorially in reviewing my *Psychology of Religion*, of having a body without a head, a mind without a heart? They had invited not infrequently international conferences. One was arranged through the instrumentality of the Y.M.C.A. in Geneva in 1929, at which scholars from different universities and countries in Europe met a small group of representatives from the United States, of whom I was spokesman. It was proposed that the meeting devote itself to the problem of how to meet the religious needs of the young men of the world. Through the several days' conference, with three sessions each day, much fellowship of thought was developed. A pretty sharp division of attitude, however, was in evidence. The Europeans, with few exceptions, wished to enter a great programme of *convincement* of the rebellious youth of the world until they should come under the sway of the traditional philosophical, theological, and institutional concepts that have commanded the allegiance of humanity through the ages. The Americans without exception, including three highest ranking officers of the Y.M.C.A., were advocates of a programme of *enrichment* of the minds of youth along nine different lines, such as, finding true spiritual values in recreation as is now done in rhythmics; the perfec-

tion of a ritual that should be wholly modern; the
cultivation of the soul of music until so-called secular
music would be religious and religious music in the
highest sense beautiful; and the vitalization of science
until the spirit of science, as the case of a Pythagoras
or a Plato or an Einstein, should become identical with
the meaning of religion. The American programme
was officially adopted. Doubtless little has ensued
in the way of its realization.

In working towards the consummation of the
character education contest heretofore mentioned, the
committee had spent most of its energy in assembling
from the world's literature those selections which,
through their high moral and religious appeal, would
have value in enriching the personality. The foundation offering the prize was more interested in the
didactic method of education and declined to publish
our extended bibliography. Defeat turned into victory
when it was made possible for us to do that work with
even greater thoroughness, and with materials drawn
from all times and countries. With funds furnished by
the universities that have sponsored the project, and
by two foundations, viz. the Institute of Social and
Religious Research and the Payne Fund, this heroic
undertaking is rapidly approaching completion. There
are eight published volumes already to our credit
and many more in the process of assembling.

UNIVERSITY OF SOUTHERN CALIFORNIA
(1 9 3 0 –   )

When the University of Southern California expressed unusual interest in this work and extended the invitation, it was a pleasure to join forces with her, and to become organically a part of her famous School of Philosophy. This resulted in the transfer of the projects and most of the equipment to Los Angeles. Part of the well-experienced staff accompanied the Institute. The cordial welcome on the part of the administration and the whole-hearted co-operation of Dr. Ralph Tyler Flewelling, Director of the School of Philosophy, as well as the encouragement of colleagues continues unabated. The assistance extended by President von KleinSmid and others in maintaining the organization of the Institute, and particularly the helpful friendliness of the late Dr. Frank C. Touton, inspires feelings of the deepest gratitude. With their co-operation and support, and through the continued generosity of the Payne Fund and other friends, it has been possible to continue our efforts and to move toward the rounding out of the work in the field of literature and towards fresh researches.

The literature project is in a distinctly significant relation to the Institute for it represents the practical realization in human personality on a large scale of the results of the researches in character. Furthermore, the selection of materials for character education is done under scientific discipline. The most recent publication of this division of the work is a series of three volumes of biographical selections. These are part of a larger scheme of analysing the entire fields of literature, art, and music, and of supplying the schools and homes of America with the best cultural materials that can be found. Special anthologies in all the main fields of literature are part of the total picture. The culmination of this programme is a set of school readers entitled *Living Through Reading*, in which not one selection is other than of the highest order when viewed as pure literature, and is at the same time morally and spiritually stimulating and enlivening.

Continuation of researches into character and its training have been facilitated through the voluntary co-operation of the divisions of Education and Psychology. The public schools and public libraries of Los Angeles have more than lived up to their traditions of being committed to the interests of Character Education since the beginning of the leadership of the former Superintendent of Schools, Mrs. Susan M. Dorsey.

SCIENTIFIC PSYCHOLOGY OF RELIGION ON A TOBOGGAN

During the first decade and a half of the present century the spirit of research in the study of religion was showing itself all about America and to some extent in Europe. It looked as if it were spontaneous, perhaps indigenous in the thought-interests of students in many centres. Soon the temper changed. Seasoned researches gave way to analytical presentations and popular discussions. Articles in the different magazines appeared voluminously. There were manifold books whose titles indicated that they were psychologies of religion. Mostly, however, they were occupied with turning the straw from old threshings, and of telling the public about a few new grains of novelty and nourishment. Periodicals devoted to the study of religion and of religious education sprang up. These contained much vitalizing talk but a modicum of wisdom based upon patient investigation. In the study of religion the condition was comparable to what would have happened in astronomy following the toilsome triumphs of Galileo, Copernicus, and Newton had students been content to poetize and philosophize on the wonders of the lawful earth and of the starry heavens.

Although genuine research subsided and creativity flattened out, there have been a few happy exceptions. Leuba's work has continued to be stimulating and valuable to the present time. Clark, in his book, *The Psychology of Religious Awakening*, shows himself to be a tireless worker and helpful interpreter. Watson, May, and Hartshorne have never ceased to work concretely and meticulously by refined methods. My determination, and that of my students, is constantly to proceed by objective methods, with evidences of faithful work showing rudely through at every point.

The fact of a slump in the science of religion can be pictured in terms of two incidents. On the occasion of the approach of the second World's Fair in Chicago, Dr. Beth of Vienna, editor of the lively periodical, *Religions Psychologie*, wrote me asking if the students of America would join those of Europe in carrying through a Congress of the Psychology of Religion to be held in connection with the Fair. I presented the possibility to each of those in the United States who had contributed greatly to this field, asking if he or some students of his had an original research to offer as a part of that congress. Not one research could I discover that was ripe for presentation, aside from a few by my own students. Beth's proposal naturally went for naught.

The second incident occurred in connection with preparations looking towards the Seventh International Philosophical Congress which was to meet at Oxford, England. At the sessions of the Sixth International Congress at Harvard, out of more than one hundred papers, mine was the only one based on the specific handling of concrete data. It was a presentation of the study of my student, Sinclair, on a comparison of three hundred "tough-minded" religiously as against an equal number of "tender-minded," that is, those who had experienced feelings of divine immediacy in communion, answer to prayer, sense of God's nearness, and so on, as against a like number who never had enjoyed such experiences. The presentation was clean-cut, based upon a statistical handling of the results of laboratory tests. The "mystics" were found to be far more suggestible, at a disadvantage in every test involving quick and accurate judgment, capable of enduring greater pain and so on through quite a revealing list. The report was sufficiently well received, particularly by the younger constituency, to warrant the proposal to look forward to a series of sessions at Oxford two years later which would be devoted to empirical studies of religion. Upon appealing to the students who might be considered reasonable expectancies, there was not one person who proposed a report.

If one should inquire after the causes of the decline of productivity in this field reasonable guesses might be forthcoming. Is it not due to the native inertia of every nerve and muscle fibre in accordance with which work was said to have been pronounced a curse? Patient research is difficult, and forensics is fun. Is not the aesthetic sense involved? Concrete data are harsh. They are rough to the skin and dry to the palate. Is there not a peculiar gratification in publicly exploiting an idea accompanied by a delicious sense of a triumphant ego? Is not the public in part to blame who hang about the workshop claiming to be mentally hungry but who are really curiosity-seekers with itching ears? Are not the economic necessities to blame that load upon the scholar heavy schedules of teaching and hurry the students into jobs before their dissertations are ripe? Perhaps the greatest trickery leading to the steady descent in the scientific curve is found in the propensity for associations and conventions. One great national association founded a third of a century ago has existed primarily for encouraging researches in this field and has turned out very little that is worthy the dignity of the word science. People feel intensely in groups. They *think* intelligently as individuals. Perhaps the one greatest cause of the decline of the output is the lack of long, patient, laborious scientific training and discipline on the part of those desiring to be masters of research.

A FORWARD GLANCE

The slowing down of the scientific work we have been describing is a cause for no discouragement. Looking across the brief span of years and the high achievements up to the present time, the story is on the whole most cheerful. When one keeps in mind that the developments in astronomy from Copernicus to Galileo occupied a century and a half, and from Copernicus to Newton two and a half centuries, and when it is observed that in physics the journey from Newton to the present time is more than two centuries, the tremendous advances in the field of the psychology of religion—with a history of only a half-century— have burst like a dream on the world.

Many of the lines of advance have been hinted in

the preceding pages. The achievement of the genetic psychology of childhood is comparable to developmental studies in botany. Functional psychology reveals conclusively that the deeper springs of life are in motivated conduct and not in thoughts about the good life. It seems now certain that the imagination is the mechanism of true release of spiritual values. The scientific measurement on a large scale of the results of certain types of training and of particular kinds of materials is a present challenge, as is also the accurate diagnosis and scientific measurement of the mentality of children and adults. There is need of assembling great literature, art, and music for stimulating the religious impulses. All these and many kindred lines of achievement give promise.

There is a great need at the present time of adequately endowed Institutes of Character Research at many of the great universities. They should have in their equipment no fewer than three types of laboratory, each fully manned. In the first place a laboratory in experimental psychology containing devices for mental measurements and for diagnosis, by means of accurate units objectively controlled. As a concrete instance, Mr. Richard E. Currier, my assistant, has learned to measure in specific units the degree of graspingness of children without their suspecting that such is happening and to know concretely the progress, if any, that is being made in transforming the responses into the disposition to share. In the very near future we shall take quite as seriously a case of selfishness or spitefulness or discourtesy in a child as we do now a case of mumps or measles, and we will correct it.

The second sort of laboratory that must come is one in bio-chemistry. There can be no longer any doubt that the behaviour of the organism conditions and sometimes determines one's conduct and entire mode of response to cultural appeals. The progress that the still imperfect science of endocrinology is now making is prophetic of the entire story.

In the third place there should be in every Institute of Character Research specialists in testing and measuring by the prevailing paper-pencil devices in certain areas of mentality. They are certain to be indispensable and permanently useful.

It will be by experimental methods that we come ultimately not only to lift out into higher significance the subtler aspects of art appreciation, of human contacts, and of inner longings after ideals, but to hold under right discipline the emotionalisms that overwhelm individuals and sweep the masses off their feet with monsoons of feeling and thin zephyrs of sentimentality. In many areas of religious experience there will never be much progress until the methods of true science put to rout the astrologers, soothsayers, and purveyors of luck charms and other cultists who falsely label themselves with the word "science."

If the promises of the last half-century are fairly realized there can be no doubt that we shall be moving speedily with the aid of clear-headed cultural engineering toward the eradication of much moral ugliness and spiritual failure and toward the realization of a better sort of humanity. We have been, of necessity, creatures at the mercy of the blind forces of nature and of human nature. If we can now create better fruits in the orchard, make more perfect mechanisms for conquering the distances, and build more perfect houses, we can also envisage the sort of humanity that is most desirable and move far towards its realization.

PRINCIPAL PUBLICATIONS

BOOKS

The Psychology of Religion. Edwin Diller Starbuck. Walter Scott, London. 1899.

Religious Education in the New World-View. Edwin Diller Starbuck. Bulletin of the Dept. of Religious Education, No. 2. Beacon Press, Boston, Mass., 1913.

Character Education Methods, The Iowa Plan. Edwin Diller Starbuck and Research Collaborators. National Capitol Press, Washington, D.C. 1922.

A Guide to Literature for Character Training. Vol. I, *Fairy Tale, Myth, and Legend.* Edwin Diller Starbuck and Staff. The Macmillan Company. 1928.

A Guide to Books for Character. Vol. II, *Fiction.* Edwin Diller Starbuck and Staff. The Macmillan Company. 1930.

The Wonder Road. Edwin Diller Starbuck and Staff, comps. The Macmillan Company. 1930.

    Vol. I. *Familiar Haunts*
    Vol. II. *Enchanted Paths.*
    Vol. III. *Far Horizons.*

Living Through Biography. Edwin Diller Starbuck and Staff, comps. World Book Company. 1936.

    Vol. I. *The High Trail.*
    Vol. II. *Actions Speak.*
    Vol. III. *Real Persons.*

CHAPTERS IN BOOKS

Chapter Three in *Moral Training in the Public Schools.* Ginn and Company. 1907.

"Character Tests and Measurements." Chapter V in *Character Education*, Bureau of Education Bulletin, No. 7. 1926. Washington, D.C.

R

"Character Education seen in Perspective," pp. 46–55, in *Building Character*. Chicago Association for Child Study and Parent Education. University of Chicago. 1928.

"Symbols in the Development of Personality." Chapter I in *Life—A Symbol*. Maurice H. Farbridge. Sherratt and Hughes, Manchester, England. 1931.

"A Philosophical View of Character," pp. 9–14; "Summary," pp. 90–2; and "Résumé," pp. 270–3, in *Interpretations of Physical Education*, Vol. III, *Character Education Through Physical Education*. J. B. Nash, editor. A. S. Barnes and Company, New York. 1932.

ARTICLES AND PAMPHLETS

In *Encyclopaedia of Religion and Ethics*. Edited by James Hastings. Charles Scribner's Sons. 1917.

Vol. II, pp. 319–21, "Backsliding."
Vol. III, pp. 693–4, "Climate."
Vol. IV, pp. 860–2, "Double-Mindedness."
Vol. IV, pp. 862–5, "Doubt."
Vol. VI, pp. 827–33, "Female Principle."
Vol. VII, pp. 397–400, "Intuitionalism."
Vol. IX, pp. 458–62, "Old Age."
Vol. XI, pp. 357–9, "Self-Expression."

"A Study of Conversion." *American Journal of Psychology*. Vol. VIII, No. 2, 1897.

"Some Aspects of Religious Growth." *American Journal of Psychology*. Vol. IX, No. 1, 1897.

"The Intimate Senses as Sources of Wisdom." *Journal of Religion*, Vol. I, No. 2, pp. 129–45, March 1921.

"Life and Confessions of G. Stanley Hall." *Journal of Philosophy*, Vol. 21, No. 6, March 13, 1924.

"Some of the Fundamentals of Character Education." *School and Society*, Vol. XX, No. 500, July 26, 1924.

"G. Stanley Hall as Psychologist." *Psychological Review*, Vol. 32, No. 2, 1925.

"An Empirical Study of Mysticism." *Proceedings of Sixth International Congress of Philosophy*, 1927.

"Methods of a Science of Character." *Religious Education*, Sept. 1927.

"Character Rating." *Child Study*, Vol. IX, No. 1, pp. 12-14, Sept. 1931.

"The Human Animal That Thinks it Thinks." *College of the Pacific-Publications in Philosophy*. College of the Pacific, Stockton, California.

"The Cultural Equivalent of Religion." *State of Calif. Dept. of Education Bulletin*, No. 12, June 15, 1932. Sacramento, California.

"New Techniques for Judging Literature." *The English Journal* (College Edition). Vol. XXIV, No. 5, May, 1935.

STUDIES

Iowa Studies in Character. Edwin Diller Starbuck, editor, Dept. of Publications, University of Iowa.

Vol. I. No. 1. *World Citizenship*. James C. Manry. 1927.

No. 2. *The Measurement of Character and Environmental Factors involved in Scholastic Success*. Frank K. Shuttleworth. 1927.

No. 3. *The Study of Religion in State Universities*. Herbert L. Searles. 1927.

No. 4. *Untruthfulness in Children: Its Conditioning Factors and its Setting in Child Nature*. W. E. Slaght. 1928.

Vol. II. No. 1. *Measurement of the Comprehension Difficulties of the Precepts and Parables of Jesus*. S. P. Franklin. 1928.

No. 2. *A Comprehensive Study of Those Who Accept Against Those Who Reject Religious Authority*. Thomas H. Howells. 1928.

No. 3. *A Comparative Study of Those Who Report the Experience of the Divine Presence and Those Who Do Not.* Robert Daniel Sinclair. 1928.

No. 4. *A Study of the Placement in the Curriculum of Selected Teaching of the Old Testament Prophets.* Ralph Thomas Case. 1930.

Vol. III. No. 1. *The Attitudes of Children Toward Law.* Earl G. Lockhart. 1930.

No. 2. *Biblical Information in Relation to Character and Conduct.* Pleasant Roscoe Hightower. 1930.

No. 3. *The Character Value of the Old Testament Stories.* George W. Beiswanger. 1930.

No. 4. *The Development of Imagination in the Pre-school Child.* Elizabeth Gordon Andrews. 1930.

Vol. IV. No. 1. *Information and Certainty in Political Opinions. A Study of University Students During a Campaign.* Harold S. Carlson. 1931.

Index

higher and historical criticism,
96, 97, 99, 100, 130, 132 ff.,
138 ff., 184, 190
Hindu Scripture, 17
Hinduism and Hindu religion,
14–17, 19, 21, 22, 27, 37, 56,
81. *See* Indian philosophy
Hinman, Prof., 24
Hodge, 230, 234
Hogg, A. G., 19
Hubbard, Elbert, 203
Hügel, von, F., 161
Human Culture Institute, 244,
245
humanism, 84, 217–219
Hume, 227
Huxley, 179
Huxley, Aldous, 30
Hylan, J. P., 230
hypocrisy in religion, 182, 183,
197, 198

Icard, M., 142
idealism, metaphysical, 24, 40, 41
imagination, 103, 228, 254
immortality, 154, 185–192, 197,
199
indenture, 76
Index, the, 143
India, 73, 76 ff., 79 ff., 82, 88,
221
India, British occupation of,
79 ff.
Indian philosophy, 19, 22, 25–
27, 37, 54, 55
Indiana University, 216 ff.
individualism, 117
infinite, the, 41
Inge, W. R., 41
inspiration of Scriptures, 133,
134, 140–143; verbal, 67

integration, personal, 39
intuition. *See* mysticism
Irenaeus, 135
Irving, E., 63

Jacks, L. P., 26, 41
James, Wm., 24, 181, 191, 204,
222, 224–227, 229, 231, 232,
234, 240
James–Lange theory, 239
Janet, 226
Jesus, 50, 57, 64–67, 71, 74, 75,
79, 81–88, 99, 108, 112, 113,
136, 137, 152, 154, 155
Jordan, D. S., 215, 235

Kant, 227
Karma, law of, 27
Kavi, the, 40
Kingsley, 216
Klein Smid, von, 248
Knight, Rachel, 204
knowledge, general, 228
knowledge, religious, 96, 98,
100, 190 ff., 228. *See* mysti-
cism

Lamentabili, decree of, 151
Lawrence, W. I., 242
League of Nations, 32
Leibniz, 24, 41, 219
Leo XIII, Pope, Encyclical, 143,
148
Leuba, 8, 173 ff., 250
liberalism, 99, 128, 129
liberty, 29, 151 ff., 177
life's values, 46 ff., 49 ff.
Loisy, A., 9, 126 ff.
love, on, 46 ff.
Lowell, 103